I know their sorrows

I know
their sorrows

David Forrester

Burns & Oates · London

First published in Britain, Ireland and associated territories in 1980 by
Burns & Oates

Copyright © 1980 David Forrester

Acknowledgments: The author and publishers are grateful to the
following for kind permission to reproduce extracts from the works
cited: Messrs W.M. Collins & Sons Ltd; Darton, Longman & Todd Ltd;
the British Medical Association; SCM Press Ltd; Macmillan Publishers Ltd;
Search Press Ltd; Ian Caws; N.C. Habel. The titles are cited in the reading
lists on pp. 78 and 139.

ISBN 0 86012 082 1
Set in IBM 11/13pt Journal by ✒Tek-Art, Croydon, Surrey
Printed and bound in Great Britain by Biddles of Guildford

Contents

Preface

There can be very few people in the world who at one time or another have not asked themselves 'Why?' in regard to some form of pain or suffering. Perhaps it was the sudden and unexpected death of someone near and dear to us, or the sight of someone we love in the throes of a painful illness. We did not understand; we only saw what seemed to us a dreadful waste and even an injustice. Perhaps we even asked ourselves; 'Why does God permit it?'

Every day, of course, we hear of suffering on a world-wide scale in the form of wars, famines, disasters and outbreaks of disease, but it is usually only when it hits us personally that we are actually shaken. In that sense it is rather like a car accident; we may read in our newspapers the alarming statistics concerning accidents on the road, but only when we are personally involved in one do we suffer shock.

Not all and not even the most common forms of suffering are dramatic or merit head-line treatment. Almost all of us know what it is to worry, to be depressed and to grow anxious. Others know what it is to suffer in their relationships with others, either at home in the family or at work. Some are acquainted with total rejection or at least alienation from others. But what about those who simply cannot face going on, and attempt suicide? What of the thousands of elderly men and women whose chief problem every day stems from feeling useless, a burden or even isolated? Who knows the suffering involved when one person exploits or discriminates against another?

C.S. Lewis once described pain as 'God's megaphone to rouse a deaf world'. This book, the title of which is taken from the Book of Exodus, chapter 3, verse 7, is intended to bring our attention to the many and various forms that pain may take in the lives of ordinary men and women, but above all to give people ground for hope.

For obvious reasons I have altered the real names and identifying backgrounds of all those involved in the incidents described. But it was the particular situations of living people which impelled me to try and seek out the Christian answer to the question 'Why?' The second part of the book examines the possibilities of Christian perfection in the state of human weakness.

This book is dedicated to the memory of my father who died of cancer and to that of my brother who was killed in action.

Our Lady, Queen of Apostles   David Forrester
Bishop's Waltham,
Feast of the Epiphany, 1979

Part I
Their sorrows

1
Death and resurrection

After suffering a brain haemorrhage, Sister Josephine lay unconscious in a coma for several days in hospital. In the meantime her relatives and the other members of her religious community maintained a vigil by her bedside and prayed continually. One evening Sister Josephine opened her eyes, attempted to smile as though wondering what all the fuss was about and murmured a gentle greeting. Not long afterwards she quietly died; an event she had steadfastly prepared for for years.

1.   Fear of death

We live in a society which shuns mention and if possible the sight of death. That does not mean that we are unaware of death. In a sense we may be morbidly interested in it to the point of obsession. Why else would editors of newspapers and producers of television programmes bring it so much to our attention every day, and sometimes brutally portray it for us? It holds people's attention even though it is not a subject of polite conversation.

What might be described as almost a conspiracy of silence on the subject extends particularly to the actual process of dying. Whereas a book or film giving graphic details of a gruesome murder or act of violence immediately receives publicity, we tend to avoid talking about the inevitable death of those in our family, including ourselves.

Less than a century ago a dying person was usually surrounded by his or her relatives, from the youngest to the oldest. Nowadays most people die alone or in the presence only of a nurse, a doctor or a priest. It might be said that in our society the kind of taboo that the Victorians placed on the public debate of sex has been transferred to death and dying.

When the Russian Orthodox Archbishop and writer, Anthony Bloom, first arrived in Britain he was immediately struck by this. In his book *School for Prayer* he remarks: 'When I arrived in England I was appalled at the British attitude to death. To die seemed to be almost an act of indecency — if you had fallen so low as to die, then there were special people who would come, undertakers, to pack and wrap you up for the funeral. Then two weeks or so later there is a nice memorial service in which one sublimates one's feelings into a kind of spiritual realm. Then I remember that I went to preach at the University Church in Cambridge on the subject of death and a priest there told me he had never seen a dead person. Why is there this morbid attitude to death? In a natural way one does not get rid of people through the back door! . . . Of course, if you have a wrong attitude to death, it becomes more and more horrible and frightening'.

As Anthony Bloom noted, funerals tend to be arranged as speedily and quietly as possible. On the other hand, they are sometimes lavish in the sense of relatives doing everything in their power to maintain the illusion that the dead person is not really dead. Apart from the elaborate devices satirized by Evelyn Waugh in his novel *The Loved One* and used by many North Americans to camouflage the realities of death, it is even more the case that we employ euphemisms and speak of the dead as having 'passed away' rather than as having actually died. The headmaster who maintained that the purpose of education was to prepare pupils for death was looked at askance and considered to have committed a breach of etiquette. A similar attitude is prevalent in our society towards the problem of grief and mourning.

2. Bereavement

In his study of grief and mourning Geoffrey Gorer maintains that in contemporary Britain 'Mourning is treated as if it were a weakness, a self-indulgence, a reprehensible bad habit instead of a psychological necessity'. And, according to Colin Murray Parkes, when making a contrast between ourselves and certain other societies, 'We do not burn our widows, we pity and avoid them'.

Given the supposedly advanced nature of the Western world, this attitude is unusually myopic, quite apart from it being un-Christian. It reveals the remarkable ignorance of many people about the nature of grief and the different stages through which a bereaved person passes, ranging from the initial numbness, followed by pining, to depression before recovery.

A refusal to face the implications of grief involves a failure to understand that human beings are also social creatures. For example, when a wife dies the husband suffers not only the loss of a companion, but usually someone upon whom he depended in a variety of other ways. On the other hand, even today the death of a husband can mean the loss of a bread-winner for a bereaved wife. The death of children can be equally if not more psychologically debilitating. In almost every case, however, the bereaved are required to fulfil new rôles at the very time when they need understanding and support, and not to be avoided as embarrassments.

If psychologists are correct in saying that resistance to change is at the root of grief, then it is here that Christians have an obligation towards their bereaved neighbours for, as John Henry Newman observed: 'In a higher world it is otherwise, but here below to live is to change, and to be perfect is to have changed often'.

It is important, however, to be aware that our obligation towards the bereaved is best fulfilled simply by being with the person concerned not by continually offering sympathy. It is not what we say at this time that is of most value, but that we are prepared to listen, to be present, and not to be embarrassed by the bereaved person's expressions of pain or even anger. If we consider crying or sobbing in these circumstances as things to be ashamed of, or as signs of weakness, then we lack true insight into the nature of grief. 'Give sorrow words', said Malcolm to Macduff. 'The grief that does not speak, knits up the o'er-wrought heart and bids it break'.

Frequently, as in our attitude to death, we find the bereavement of others something we prefer to avoid. When it is not possible to avoid grief in another, we often complain of not knowing what to say, we restrict our conversation to trivialities and usually we feel unable to do more than pity the bereaved person — an emotion least helpful to the one grieving.

In their daily lives and routines Christians as much as others in the western world are governed by time, measured in the sense of having things to do. Around us there is an emphasis on activity and doing rather than on

14

being. This is so much so that even those occasions of intense joy, happiness and achievement seem inevitably to pass. We seem unable to hold on to them. Nothing seems to last. On the other hand is that truly reality? Anthony Bloom also says: 'The Christian is like someone who lives in three dimensions in a world in which the majority of people live in two. People who live freely and within a dimension of eternity will always find that something is wrong, they will always find themselves being the odd man out . . . If you really live in three dimensions and do not simply live in two and imagine the third, then life will be full and meaningful'.

3. The Christian approach

For the Christian death is not the destruction of true achievement, of true love, of all that is good. The reason for this course is our belief in the Resurrection.

Although we may not be in a position to know the exact nature of what happened in Christ's tomb on the first Easter Day one thing is certain. It transformed a frightened and dismayed group of disciples so that they won enough confidence not only to preach about the event, but to defy the Jewish establishment and the authorities of the whole Roman Empire. Moreover their experience of the resurrection lives on in the Church as a community of believers meeting Christ almost two thousand years later in prayer and the sacraments. And Christians today still risk their lives in eastern Europe, Asia, parts of Africa, South America and elsewhere. Like the first apostles, they do not pretend that death is something to be ignored. What makes them so different from us?

Jesus's disciples believed that the personal life of the

15

Jesus they knew had died on the cross had been transformed into a new mode of existence; one which transcended the limitations of this world. Even so they were able to recognize him as the same person they had known before his death. Moreover he did not simply become a ghost but possessed a glorified body; he had undergone the resurrection. It is a Christian's belief that what occurred to Jesus will happen to all those who believe in him; a process essentially set in motion with baptism. It is the basis of Christian hope: 'If there is no resurrection of the dead', St Paul told the people of Corinth, 'Christ himself cannot have been raised, and if Christ has not been raised then our preaching is useless and your believing is useless . . . If our hope in Christ has been for this life only, we are the most unfortunate of all people' (1 Cor. 15:12-14).

Is our lack of faith the reason why so many of us fear death, shun mention of the subject and do not want to take it into account in our everyday lives? In all probability we spend more time concerned with other things, ranging from work to leisure activities, none of which is as inevitable as death. Some people even talk of their need on occasion to 'kill time'. They cannot bear inactivity and fear a state which leaves them opportunity to think.

When plans or projects of our own devising and on which we set store are capable of realization, they usually command our immediate interest and concern. The one event, however, which is certain to be realized often fails to be taken into account. That is the basic difference between so many of us and really aware Christians. On the other hand, as Newman remarked: 'When we lie on the bed of death, what will it avail us to have been rich, or great, or fortunate, or honoured, or

16

influential? All things will then be vanity. Well, what this world will be understood by all to be then (the last day), such is it felt to be by the Christian now. He looks at things as he then will look at them . . .' (*Parochial & Plain Sermons*, vol. V).

This Christian attitude of mind is vividly illustrated in the story told by Michael Hollings in his book *I will be there* of the couple who had married in middle life and who were devoted to each other. The husband apparently had a bad heart and over a period suffered severe heart failure. The couple faced this calmly and together. Eventually the man entered hospital for the last time, in desperate pain and dying, but fully conscious. When the doctors said they were giving him an injection to ease him. His reply was: 'I want to go. I want to be with God! I'm sorry, love, I love you very much, but I want to go to God'. His wife stayed all night by his bedside, and said later that they had a peaceful night, quietly talking, or in prayer and silence. Early in the morning the man died. Since that time, says Michael Hollings, the wife has lived on alone in the physical world, but very much alive to Christ's words: 'He who believes in me will never die'.

How can we begin now to cultivate this attitude of mind towards death, instead of finding it a subject of embarrassment, fear, or something to avoid facing? Newman was of the opinion that if as Christians we carried around with us the truth that 'The time is short' then our whole outlook would change. We would be acutely aware that ultimately not only are the things in which we take refuge bound to pass away, but so are our forebodings, anxieties, griefs, resentments, pains, and disappointments. But let us look now at the lives of at least two of the original followers of Jesus who were so affected by the events of the first Easter.

4.   The influence of example

Paradoxically, for ordinary people one of the reassuring facts concerning Peter, the leader of the apostles, is the 'imperfections' in his character. These are of tremendous value when we consider our own weaknesses and fears and on occasion begin to doubt whether we shall ever as it were make the grade in God's eyes. Such was the extent of Peter's extravagances, when examined in detail, that we could be forgiven for wondering why Jesus obviously selected him as the leader of his followers in the first place.

When Jesus appeared on the shore of the Sea of Tiberias after his resurrection, and seven of the disciples were out fishing, what was Peter's spontaneous reaction when John the Beloved declared: 'It is the Lord'! We are told that Peter 'who had practically nothing on, wrapped his cloak round him and jumped into the water'. Whereas the others made for the shore by boat, Peter leapt into the sea. Many 'common-sense' people would declare this to be a sign of impetuosity if not of recklessness.

On a previous occasion, when he jumped out of his boat to reach Jesus, Peter became a victim of doubts and fears and began to sink beneath the waves. Because of this, Jesus chided him as a 'man of little faith'.

Even after his famous and moving confession of faith in Jesus as the Christ, the Son of the living God, Peter was almost immediately rebuked as 'Satan' for trying to dissuade Jesus from the way of the cross and persuade him to take a more ambitious and worldly path.

In truth, Peter's protest at the Last Supper when Jesus announced that he intended to wash his disciples' feet, his anger in Gethsemane resulting in his cutting off the

18

ear of the servant of the High Priest, his cowardice in denying any knowledge of Jesus before the cock crowed three times, and his later falling in with Judaeo-Christian prejudices about the need for Gentile Christians to be circumcized (ending in Peter being rebuked to his face by Paul), are all incidents of tremendous comfort to the rest of us. This comfort is increased when we appreciate that Peter, in spite of his failings, could be equally and powerfully repentant.

Who else but Peter, after learning that unless he submitted to having his feet washed by Jesus at the Last Supper he could have no further part with the Master, would have demanded that Jesus should also wash his hands and his head? Unique Peter may have been in his boldness, but his dismay and bursting into tears when he understood the extent of his denying all knowledge of Christ are surely something we can all share.

Even though all these events may be attributed to the largeness of Peter's heart when opened up by the dynamism of the relationship he enjoyed with the Jesus who was visible in Galilee and Jerusalem, they were not the end of the story.

It was for a risen Christ that Peter travelled to the centre of the Roman Empire to preach the Gospel. When his turn came to die, what other than his utter belief in the resurrection, conviction that Jesus was God's Son, and awareness of his own unworthiness to follow the Master so closely, made him ask to be crucified up-side-down?

In all this it is important to read and ponder on what Newman wrote over a century ago about the major influences on human beings: 'The heart is commonly reached, not through the reason, but through the imagination, by means of direct impressions, by the testimony of facts and events, by history, by description. Persons influence us, voices melt us. Looks subdue us, deeds inflame us. Many a man will live and die upon a dogma: no man will be a martyr for a conclusion. A conclusion is but an opinion ... No one, I say, will die for his own calculations: he dies for realities . . .' (*Grammar of Assent*).

This was true not only of Peter but of the beloved disciple, John. In John's gospel we are told that when Mary Magdalen informed Peter and John that the stone sealing Christ's tomb had been moved John, 'running faster than Peter, reached the tomb first . . . he saw and he believed'. For John, the resurrection was clearly not — as for so many — a stumbling block. Many people are able to accept Jesus as an inspired teacher, an ideal, and an example to follow, but for a Christian the acid test is acceptance of the resurrection.

From John's reaction at finding the empty tomb it would seem that to believe it is necessary to love. Love brings comprehension and conviction. Love which gave John the insight so many of us lack. This is conveyed movingly in the first epistle of John: 'Something which existed since the beginning, that we have heard and we have seen with our eyes; that we watched and touched with our hands; the Word, who is life — this is our Subject. That life was made visible: we saw it and we are giving our testimony, telling you of eternal life' (1 John 1:3).

The love which all the apostles had for the person of Jesus accounts for the total absence of nostalgia in the New Testament writings. They are incomprehensible unless we appreciate that they were written in the light of the resurrection. They never offer any sign that Jesus's disciples ever once ached or pined for him to be with them again in the earthly way he once had been; similarly, they are imbued with what Newman calls 'realities'.

For the first disciples and for committed Christians ever since, these 'realities' are that God has accomplished and revealed his definitive act of salvation in Christ's incarnation, death and resurrection.

In the technical language of a theologian such as Alfaro, this means regarding Christ as the 'eschaton': as one whose existence in history was directed to transcending history. As a man like ourselves, Jesus was destined to die; as the Son of God made man he was destined to pass through death to life with God beyond history. Moreover God calls us to have faith in Christ. Our belief in Christ as our 'eschaton' enables us to share in the divine life through the presence of the Holy Spirit, for 'God became man that men might become gods'.

In Christ we learn to know the Father and to share the love of Jesus for his Father, but it is through the Holy Spirit that in a sense we also become the sons of the Father. As St Paul wrote to the people of Rome: 'You have received the spirit of adoption, whereby we cry, Abba, Father. The Spirit itself beareth witness with our spirit, that we are the children of God' (Rom. 8:15, 16). To the Galatians Paul repeats this message that we are the sons of God (Gal. 4:6).

Our response to this call of God to have faith in his Son is the basis of Christian hope. According to Alfaro, 'Christian hope is "existence in exodus"; that is, a going out of oneself, renouncing any guarantee of salvation provided by human reckoning, in order to trust solely in the divine promise: a breaking of the moorings of all assurance in oneself and in the world and a tossing of the anchor into the bottomless depths of the mystery of God in Christ'.

But why do so many people fail to answer the call to have faith in Christ? Perhaps people nowadays have

21

become too self-sufficient in their outlook and consider
that they no longer need Christ. In a supposedly more
sophisticated and scientific age, many certainly find
miracles (for example) and the resurrection (*par
excellence*) subjects of embarrassment.

5.   *The purpose of miracles: the awakening of faith*

Unlike the original makers of the gospel tradition, we
(in the West at least) live at a time when belief in God as
the source of all power is at a low ebb. For biblical
writers God was not only personal, active, and living,
but the One from whom all power (including earthly
political power) derived. He was also regarded as the Lord
of nature in the sense of being the creator and sustainer
of the world and the Lord of history. Miracle stories
therefore posed no problem to biblical writers, whether
of the Old or New Testament. In St Mark's gospel, for
instance, some 209 verses (or one third of the gospel)
have to do either directly or indirectly with miracles.
These are inseparable from the essential gospel message;
they are not just an extra which may be disregarded at
will. They are part of the very basis, and account for the
biblical conviction that with God all things are possible
(Gen. 18:4; Jer. 32:17; Mk 10:27).

In the New Testament the resurrection was regarded
as the supreme manifestation of God's power at work. It
is no accident, as Alan Richardson has pointed out in his
book on the miracle stories, that both the miracle of the
crossing of the Red Sea in the Old Testament and the
resurrection of Jesus in the New were 'deliverances in
history from outside history'; events man could not have
achieved on his own. What is more, without the 'sign' of
the crossing of the Red Sea there would have been no

Jewish religion as we know it — and no Israel and no Old Testament. Equally, without the Resurrection of Jesus there would have been no Christian religion, no Church and no New Testament.

For more than a few today the miracles performed by Jesus during his earthly ministry are a stumbling-block to belief. For some they are useful as 'evidence' that Jesus is the Son of God; but this notion of 'evidence' is a comparatively modern idea, and it is not the reason why they are included in the Gospel. For others, the miracle stories are attempts to indicate Jesus's superiority as a 'wonder worker'. For yet others, they are simply illustrations of Jesus's tender and caring disposition. In fact, according to Alan Richardson, 'the object of the miracle stories was *to awaken saving faith* in the Person of Christ'.

In this connexion, it is important to appreciate that Jesus is never recorded as having indulged in wonder-working as a display. He did not perform miracles to prove to others who he was, and he was highly indignant with those who sought them for their own sake (Mk 8:12). Furthermore, Jesus invariably showed considerable reserve when it came to miracles, since he did not wish them to be treated in isolation from the true nature of faith and his teaching. 'What do you want me to do for you?' Jesus asked the blind man near Jericho. 'Sir', he replied, 'let me see again'. Jesus said to him, 'Receive your sight. Your *faith* has saved you'. And instantly his sight returned and he followed him praising God . . . (Lk. 18:41-43).

It is interesting that the word 'miracle' never occurs throughout the entire New Testament. Instead there are words such as 'mighty deeds', 'works' and 'signs'; and where Jesus is concerned there is an emphasis on the need for faith. This is made plain in the case of Martha, the sister of Lazarus.

For centuries poor Martha, who in Jesus' words 'worried and fretted' about so many things, has been compared unfavourably with her sister Mary. During Jesus's visit to their home, whereas Mary sat down at the Lord's feet and listened to him speaking, Martha was distracted with all the serving and indeed asked Jesus to tell her sister to lend a hand. Throughout the ages, as a consequence of this, Mary has been held up as an example of the contemplative way of life. Christ's words, 'Martha, Martha, you worry and fret about so many things and yet few are needed, indeed only one', have been mistakenly interpreted as meaning that he was deliberately drawing a contrast between life-styles and favouring the contemplative way. Scripture scholars now inform us that what Jesus actually was doing was emphasizing the need for faith as the one thing necessary, no matter who we are or what we are doing.

Lack of faith is not a new phenomenon. But the self-sufficient humanism of modern people — the deadly enemy of biblical religion — certainly makes it that much harder for us to experience the miracles of Jesus (and especially his resurrection) as a means of awakening faith. Until we return to regarding God as the Lord of creation and history in the biblical manner and discover Christ as 'Christ the power of God' (1 Cor. 1:24), we shall continue to merit the strictures directed by St Paul against the people of Corinth: 'Make no mistake about it', wrote Paul. 'If any one of you thinks of himself as wise, in the ordinary sense of the word, then he must learn to be a fool before he really can be wise. Why? Because the wisdom of this world is foolishness to God. As scripture says: "The Lord knows wise men's thoughts:

he knows how useless they are: or again: God is not convinced by the arguments of the wise".' (1 Cor. 3:18-20).

6. Seeing the resurrection as relevant for the present. The rôle of the Holy Spirit.

Perhaps many people mistakenly restrict resurrection to the belief that Jesus was alive after being dead. If so, they fail to grasp that Christ's resurrection is an event which can affect them personally. Just as they are reluctant to take their own inevitable death into account in living their daily earthly lives, so they find it hard to conceive that what occurred to Jesus two thousand years ago can influence what happens to them now. They do not see the resurrection as the dawn of a new age, the beginning of a fundamentally different era in history, after which nothing is ever again the same, they do not realize that (according to St Paul) even creation was affected by it.

Those of us who call ourselves Christian may be partly responsible for others failing to respond in faith to Christ. They do not obtain from us a strong enough impression that Christ is a living reality to us and that we can be changed by his resurrection. As Nietzsche once observed: 'If only Christians would look more as though they had been saved!' Instead, we too often merit St Francis de Sales' description of pious folk as those who look as though they had been living on a diet of sour fruit. Do we really behave as though to exist is to go to meet our death? Because we are Christians, do we regard the whole of life as a frontier of hope?

If resurrection is either restricted to what happened to Christ on Easter Day two thousand years ago, or conceived as something that will happen to us only at some time after our death, it is small wonder that modern man not only fears and shuns death but finds the whole matter of resurrection beyond belief. We have to convince ourselves that, as a result of the death and resurrection of Christ, we are already being transformed through the working of the Holy Spirit, and that this is a foretaste of the ultimate resurrection.

Only in comparatively recent times have western Christians become more aware of the Holy Spirit as a living and vital Person in their lives. Even in the eastern Orthodox Church, the doctrine of the Holy Spirit is acknowledged to have the character of a secret, partially revealed tradition. This fact and the reason for it were noted by Gregory Nazianzus, one of the four great Greek doctors of the Church, as long ago as the fourth century: 'The Old Testament', wrote Gregory, 'manifested the Father plainly, the Son obscurely. The New Testament revealed the Son and hinted at the divinity of the Holy Spirit. Today the Spirit dwells among us and makes himself more clearly known. For it was not safe, when the Godhead of the Father was not yet acknowledged, plainly to proclaim the Son; nor when that of the Son was not yet received to burden us further . . . with the Holy Spirit . . . but rather that by gradual additions, and, as David says, goings up and advances and progress from glory to glory, the light of the Trinity might shine upon the more illuminated . . .' (Migne, *P.G.* XXXVI, pp.161-4).

In the Old Testament there is a gradual revelation of the 'Spirit of God' as an instrument of divine action in both nature and within human beings. At the creation God's Spirit is seen as the source of life, hovering over the face of the waters (Gen. 1:2) and quickening life in the inert body of the first man (Gen. 2:7). He is also present in the artistic ability of Bezalel and Oholiab

26

(Ex. 36:1), the victories of Joshua (Deut. 34:9), and the deeds of such judges as Othniel, Gideon, Jephthah and Samson (Jdg. 3:10; 6:34; 11:29; 14:6; 15:14). Job proclaims the faith of Israel when he says: 'It was the Spirit of God which made me', and Ezekiel regarded possession of such a Spirit as essential for his prophetic mission (Ez. 11:24-25). It was generally believed that the looked-for Messiah King would possess the Spirit to the full (Is. 42:1), and that the messianic age would witness an enormous outpouring of the Spirit (Joel 3:1-5).

Within the synoptic gospels of the New Testament we discover that understanding of the Holy Spirit went a stage further. Continuity with the Old Testament ideas is maintained by reference to 'overshadowing' by the Holy Spirit, such as in Gabriel's message to Mary, and by reference to a 'cloud', as at the Transfiguration and Ascension of Christ. Both these expressions would have reminded Judaeo-Christians of the descent of a cloud and of the overshadowing of the Tent of Witness in the Book of Exodus; they could not have failed to think of the Divine Presence or *Shekinah*. Even so there is development by mention of the fact that the same Spirit descended on Jesus at his baptism (Mk 1:10), supported him against Satan in the wilderness (Mk 1:12), and was present from the beginning of Jesus's ministry (Mk 4:14).

The writer of the fourth gospel speaks most fully of the Spirit as the 'Advocate' and 'another Paraclete' or intercessor, counsellor, support and protector. In the fourth chapter of John, the Holy Spirit is described as the 'Spirit of truth', and elsewhere as the one who would reveal and inspire the true worship of God as opposed to the devil, 'the father of lies'. In the last discourses the Holy Spirit is described by Jesus as the One who intercedes with God the Father, and the One who would teach the disciples how Jesus was the Messiah who fulfilled the Scriptures, as well as instruct them in the meaning of Jesus's words, actions and signs.

From the Acts of the Apostles we are all familiar with how a mighty wind 'filled the whole house' and how the 'divine fire split into tongues and hovered over the apostles' heads'. It was one of the functions of the apostles to convey the gift of the Spirit to others by the laying on of hands (Acts 15:25).

It may be that, unlike the first apostles who were so to speak set ablaze in a dynamic missionary spirit at Pentecost, we have attempted to tame the Spirit. Perhaps we have turned the fire into a cosy fire-place and give it the name of 'religion'. Certainly many of us rarely consider the Holy Spirit as a person capable of 'washing away our squalors, watering our arid souls, bending our stubbon wills, kindling our frozen hearts and directing our straying steps'.

What makes St Paul's writings on the Holy Spirit fundamentally important is that in them it is often impossible to separate the Holy Spirit and Christ. For Paul, the Christian life is life 'in the Spirit' or life 'in Christ', and this is invariably and basically different to life 'in the flesh'. For Paul, the presence of the Holy Spirit makes the Christian's body the Temple of God (1 Cor. 3:16; 6:17). As in John, the Holy Spirit is our intercessor with the Father (Rom. 8:26). He also divides his gifts among men as he chooses (1 Cor. 12:11) and the fruits of the Spirit are 'love, joy, peace, patience, kindness, goodness, trustfulness, gentleness and self-control' (Gal. 5:22). For our present purpose, it is vital to note that when Paul wrote to the people of Corinth he taught that the Spirit will raise up our bodies as 'spiritual bodies' in the likeness of Christ's resurrection (1 Cor. 15:42-44).

In view of this teaching on how we may be transformed by the working of the Holy Spirit (provided we have faith), can an aware Christian really believe that not only our own but shared experiences of purest joy, love, intense happiness and real achievement pass away because of death? Undoubtedly they often live on in the lives of others, and sometimes have a permanent effect and possibly eternal significance.

Sister Josephine, the nun mentioned at the very beginning of this chapter, certainly died, but since virtually the whole of her earthly life had been spent in the service not only of her religious community but of the wide city area in which she lived, her influence long afterwards is still immeasurable.

To those who measure by worldly standards and see only through worldly eyes, Sister Josephine probably seemed to be only an ordinary nun. The truth is she had an unusual gift: that of proving by her life of faith how extraordinary the apparently ordinary may be. She fitted remarkably Newman's description of the Christian as someone who has neither fear nor hope about this world. Her life conveyed precisely what Gerald Vann summed up as true holiness: 'We shall never understand the Christian ideal of holiness unless we understand its *humanness.* It does not mean being always in the clouds; it does not mean being forever rapt in mystical vision and forgetting to cook the dinner, to darn the clothes. It does not mean being so absorbed in God as to forget man'. At the same time she had the one thing necessary, and was therefore fully prepared to die.

After encountering such people as Sister Josephine, and the many people like her who never merit head-line treatment in worldly terms, we are made to wonder who really are the dead: people such as her, or fairly

29

representative modern people who 'live' in a modern way. Is the person whose life is that of a consumer, a killer of time, and someone lacking in faith truly alive? What of those of us who sit in front of television programmes and are often helpless in spite of our acknowledged boredom? How 'alive' are those indifferent to suffering, violence and injustice? How many in the quest for power, position, promotion and status symbols are already 'dead'?

7. Attitudes contrasted

Not long ago a priest gave a lift in his car to a hitch-hiker, a young man of nineteen. The priest asked him what he did for a living and what interests he had. The young man said he had been expelled from two schools, had quarrelled with his 'old man' at home, had idled at the technical college to which he had gone, and then had worked in several types of factory. He was now on his way to join the merchant navy. He said he had three interests in life: engines, drink and girls.

After that the priest asked him what he thought was the purpose of life and immediately the young man became embarrassed. He quietly admitted that he didn't believe in God and in his own words didn't know what to make of it all. What was more he didn't like thinking about it. He said that all he wanted was to be happy.

In saying this the young man was not so unlike any average man or woman. If pressed to explain what they mean by happiness, they usually equate it with 'having a good time'. This might mean having a pint at the local with their mates, watching their favourite team play soccer, going to bingo or playing bridge with their friends, having a flutter on the horses or playing a round of golf, watching Top of the Pops or spending Saturday night at a disco, or simply putting their feet up with the Sunday papers. Only a puritan would object on principle to any of these things, but they are a long way removed from what St Paul intended when he wrote to the people of Philippi on the subject of happiness. He said: 'I want you to be happy, always happy in the Lord; I repeat, what I want is your happiness'. Clearly when Paul refers to 'being happy in the Lord' he is concerned with an inner happiness; something the young hitch-hiker had not yet discovered.

When the priest returned from his journey by car, having dropped the young man off at his destination, he was greeted with the news that in his absence a sixty-two-year-old man in the parish had died. For the previous four years, this man had been in and out of hospital suffering from leukaemia. The difference between the old man and the young hitch-hiker was not only one of age, nor one simply of sickness and health, but basically one of outlook. The man who had died had been deeply acquainted with suffering. Over the previous four years he had experienced what Paul Tillich referred to when he said: 'The depth . . . of suffering is the door, the only door, to the depth of truth. The fact is obvious. It is comfortable to live on the surface so long as it remains unshaken. It is painful to break away from it and descend into unknown ground . . .' (*The Shaking of the Foundations*).

Furthermore, in the midst of his suffering the slowly dying man had come to realize the inner meaning of Christ's words, 'I am the Resurrection and the Life', for he became the kind of Christian described by Anthony Bloom as 'someone who lives in three dimensions in a world in which the majority of people live in two'; the third dimension being that of eternity.

31

2

Euthanasia versus
proper care of the dying

*Joseph is sixty-four years old. Until recently he led a full
and active life. By profession he was a skilled engineer.
The use of the past tense here is deliberate. Joseph has
lately been diagnosed as suffering from cerebral dystrophy
or gradual deterioration of the brain. A few months ago
he was happily looking forward to retirement and the
leisure this would bring him to pursue his many hobbies.
Now and increasingly as time goes on Joseph is becoming
utterly helpless. He is incontinent, can no longer wash
or feed himself, and has lost both his power of speech
and ability to write. No one can tell just how much
Joseph understands of the world around him any more.
In the meantime he simply sits staring vacantly into space
or when he attempts to move causes chaos by his total
lack of mental and physical co-ordination. The doctors
are of the opinion that Joseph's condition can only
steadily worsen.*

Confronted with a person such as Joseph, many would
find incredible all Christian talk of experiencing the
eternal in the here-and-now, or of death being the thresh-
old to a new dimension of life through faith in Christ.
What about compassion? they ask. Wouldn't it be more

humane and loving, they inquire, to put Joseph out of his misery by administering a painless but lethal drug?

Because Joseph is typical of thousands of predominantly elderly people in our society who suffer from one form or other of an apparently incurable mental or physical illness, euthanasia is no longer simply a matter of academic interest or discussion. The late Cardinal Heenan, commenting on the Lane Report on abortion, remarked that legal euthanasia was a short but logical step from legal abortion.

The Euthanasia Society (known since 1969 as the Voluntary Euthanasia Society) was founded as long ago as 1935. In 1936 and 1969 bills were introduced in the House of Lords to legalize euthanasia. On the last occasion, forty per cent of the Lords members voted in favour; clearly this is not an out-of-date issue.

Perhaps a statement typical of those made by advocates of euthanasia was that of Mary Stocks, the well-known broadcaster, author and life peer, in the spring 1972 edition of *Age Concern Today*. Baroness Stocks wrote, with reference to the rights of old people: 'There is another right I should like them to have — and which I should like to have myself — I mean the right to die when they are ready to go. The right, when in full possession of their wits, to sign a paper saying: When I am no longer a thinking human being or when I am moving towards the end of an incurable illness, I want a doctor to put me to sleep and to see to it that I don't wake up'.

Current public interest in the subject has been shown by the staging in London during 1978 of two plays, *Whose Life Is It Anyway* and *Sentenced to Life,* both of which deal with euthanasia. Before discussing the Christian attitude to the matter, however, it is important to define more precisely what we mean by euthanasia.

1. Definitions

Originally the word 'euthanasia', from the Greek, signified a dignified and honourable death, carrying connotations of a physician assuaging and alleviating the agonies of death by medication. Only in the present century has the word taken on its present meaning, suggesting the direct and painless killing of a patient considered beyond recovery.

Karl Binding and Alfred Hoche, in Germany in 1920, proposed the term euthanasia to include in addition the premeditated and large-scale extermination of people considered socially and economically 'unfit', such as the mentally ill and the crippled. This was precisely what Hitler practised in addition to his extermination of several million Jews. Even today, when almost all present-day advocates of euthanasia deplore Binding's and Hoche's proposals, one frequently comes across the term 'useless lives'; a phrase suggesting that certain individuals have lives supposedly no longer worth living.

At this point it is important to distinguish between 'negative euthanasia' and 'positive euthanasia'. Negative euthanasia signifies the planned omission of treatments which would probably prolong life, whereas positive euthanasia is defined as the institution of 'therapies' designed to promote death. This latter is sometimes also called 'mercy killing' and is largely motivated, say its proposers, by compassion.

Equally vital is the need to differentiate between negative euthanasia (implying the cessation of treatments so that a patient can die), and dispensing the 'extraordinary' means of prolonging life. Even before the second Vatican Council declared in section 27 of its *Pastoral Constitution on the Church in the Modern World* that euthanasia was an 'infamy', Pope Pius XII had made this distinction in a discourse to doctors (on 24 November 1957). In an age when it is not unusual for a person to end his days with tubes in every orifice and needles in his veins, and to be attached to a heart or lung machine, the Pope had spoken approvingly of families who requested of doctors that respirators should be removed to allow a patient, already virtually dead, to die in peace.

Debate concerning the use of 'extraordinary' means of prolonging life obviously raises the related question of how we should define 'death' and the 'moment of death'. Before heart transplanting, medical science was already aware of the importance of the cerebral cortex as the centre of consciousness and voluntary action. It is 'brain death' that indicates the end of a person's earthly life, and artificial methods of sustaining life in the heart, lungs, kidney and liver should therefore cease once brain death has taken place.

Definitions are necessary if only to make clear to those in favour of euthanasia that there is nothing in Catholic teaching to indicate disapproval of treatments whose *direct* purpose is the suppression of pain and anxiety, even though the shortening of a terminal illness might be foreseen. Catholics are not of the same mind as Christian Scientists who believe that nature in such a case should always be permitted to take its course, nor do Catholics agree with Jehovah Witnesses who consider even blood transfusions to be immoral.

2. *The medical profession*

The rôle of the medical profession has to be considered in any discussion concerning death, but especially the possible use of euthanasia. But first we should try to find out of the views of doctors and nurses themselves.

In 1972 C.E. Dent reported in the periodical *Contact* the views of the staff of a British teaching hospital. Four members of staff supported the Euthanasia Society's aims, and fifty were against them. Fifty-two out of fifty-four believed that dying patients should be given relief from pain and distress, even though it might shorten their lives. Fifty-three out of fifty-four considered that treatment should be withheld from a dying person if shortening his life was considered merciful. Forty-seven out of fifty-four were on the whole satisfied with British law as it stands in regard to dying patients.

Three years before C.E. Dent's survey, the American physician R.H. Williams had also published a report based on a survey among chairmen of medical schools in the USA, and among members of the Association of American Physicians.

For this report, entitled *Our rôle in the generation, modification and termination of life,* 344 questionnaires were sent out and there were 337 replies. Of those who replied eighty-seven per cent were in favour of negative euthanasia and eighty per cent indicated that they practised it. As to positive euthanasia, Williams' inquiry revealed that only very few doctors voted in favour of it.

It would appear, simply from the practical point of view, that if legislation were introduced permitting so-called voluntary euthanasia it would bring more problems than solutions. This is certainly the view of B.P. Bliss and A.G. Johnson, the authors of *Aims and Motives in Clinical Medicine* (1975), and of Hugh Trowell, the Chairman of the BMA panel on euthanasia and author of *The Unfinished Debate on Euthanasia* (1973). Perhaps doctors are more aware than ourselves why euthanasia should not be made a matter of law,

37

irrespective of any so-called 'well-determined conditions' such as those in the 1969 Act attempting to make it legal, such conditions are the decision of the patient having to be free and spontaneous, and an interim period of thirty days between a statement of intent and its execution.

In his book *Dying* (second edition, reprinted 1976), Professor John Hinton asks the following questions. What about the possibility of a mistake in diagnosis? How much would fear of being a burden cloud a patient's decision? At what point of an incurable illness would it be reasonable to recommend euthanasia? Exactly how much suffering would a person face before his life was curtailed? How close to death should a patient be before euthanasia is introduced? Would 'severe chronics', such as people with already severely curtailed lives and those with progressive paralysis, be included? Who would be considered suitable referees to issue the order to the doctors.

Whereas it may be the task of advocates of euthanasia to answer these questions, Christians must know where they stand.

3. Christians confronting death

At this point it is instructive to return to the situation of Joseph mentioned at the beginning of this chapter. Many people observing Joseph, and certainly those who are aware of the active life he was leading not so very long ago, would now pityingly and inhumanely describe him as a 'vegetable'. This, however, is too facile.

Although it would appear that Joseph is rapidly deteriorating to the point of total mental disintegration, he still shows panic when his wife, Maria, is absent for any length of time. She is resolved to nurse Joseph at home, whatever the cost to her own health, for the remainder of her life.

The explanation for Maria's behaviour is not hard to find: it is based on a love which involves total giving not only in theory but in practice. If any one should be so rash as to compare Joseph with a suffering animal, and to point out to Maria that it is customary to put animals out of their misery, they would probably bitterly regret their temerity.

Long before Joseph became ill, he and Maria had often experienced the fact that human life on earth is not always sweetness and light. When they exchanged their marriage vows their love was rooted in the accepted belief that it was for better or worse, for richer or poorer, in sickness and in health.

Like all mature Christians, they did not for one moment believe that suffering in itself was good or necessarily ennobling; they appreciated the havoc it might cause (which in their case it is causing), but they also tied the flag of endurance to their main-mast, Christ. Not endurance for its own sake nor in the Stoic fashion, but endurance akin to fidelity; a trustfulness in God which precludes any premature anticipation of what God intends. Both love and endurance are, in Maria's eyes (and in those of all Christians like her), better fulfilled by caring attendance of Joseph in his suffering and dying.

If we drop an empty bucket into the sea and then retrieve it, we learn a great deal from its contents. We may measure the contents' temperature, analyze how much salt it contains and estimate the quality and quantity of water in the bucket. Even so, what would such a bucket of salt water tell us of the hidden depths of the oceans, the storms which sweep across them, and the teeming fish and vegetable life way below the surface? Almost nothing. It is the same with God and his purposes.

If Jesus had not become incarnate, how little we would

know of God. We might find him in nature, we could worship him, and we could pray to him, but if Jesus his Son had not come to earth and among other things have endured suffering, how much less we would have penetrated to God's love for us and the true response to pain, sickness and suffering.

Not long ago a priest was summoned to the intensive care unit of a chest hospital in a large city. He had been called to the bedside of a man suffering from acute bronchitis whose state was complicated by damage to his heart. Because the man had no reserves to call upon, the doctors' diagnosis and prognosis were not hopeful; they were quite the reverse.

While the priest was hearing the man's confession, anointing him as part of the sacrament of the sick, and giving him Holy Communion, the man's family were advised to prepare themselves for the possibility of his death. The dying man however had only one concern after receiving the sacrament: from his bed he kept whispering to his wife: 'Don't be afraid'. In other words, he was concerned about her, not himself. He had made his own the words of Christ: 'Do not be afraid of those who kill the body but cannot kill the soul: fear him rather who can destroy both body and soul in hell . . . Every hair on your head has been counted. So there is no need to be afraid; you are worth more than hundreds of sparrows' (Mt. 10:28-31).

In his own way, and prompted by love for his wife, the sick man in hospital was echoing Jesus's counsel. He was also attempting to reassure her that if he died he would be even closer to her than when on earth. St John Chrysostom put this succinctly in relation to Christ when he said: 'He whom we love and lose is no longer where he was before. He is now wherever we are'.

40

But much of the debate on euthanasia is concerned with what is called 'freedom to choose'. It is indeed one of the glories of the human race that man does have free-will. Nevertheless it is not the only quality he possesses or the only right he may exercise. Still less does freedom to choose mean either doing what one likes or doing anything at all provided it does not hurt any one else. Christians at least, believing humans to have been made in God's image and through faith in Christ to be capable of becoming adopted children, accept that though free they also belong to God.

Christians also believe with St Paul that our main task is not to try for perfection by our own efforts but for a perfection that comes through faith in Christ. As St Paul told the people of Philippi; 'All I want is to know Christ and the power of his resurrection and to share his suffering by reproducing the pattern of his death. That is the way I can hope to take my place in the resurrection of the dead' (Phil. 3:10-11).

Belonging to God therefore necessarily means that a Christian does not share the humanist motto: 'I am the master of my fate. I am the captain of my soul'. True, freedom is bound up with redemption and death is the ultimate occasion for faith and choosing between God and self, even though adherence, as in the case of Joseph, may be utterly passive.

Death for a Christian therefore has to do with God. Was not that the way that Jesus himself 'learned obedience'? It is this notion that pervades Teilhard de Chardin's prayer: 'At that moment when I feel I am losing hold of myself and am absolutely passive within the hands of the great unknown forces that have formed me . . . O God grant that I may understand that it is You (provided only my faith is strong enough) who are

41

painfully parting the fibres of my being in order to penetrate to the very marrow of my substance and bear me away within Yourself' (*Le Milieu Divin*).

Not only Christians are opposed to euthanasia. Viktor Frankl, the author of *The Doctor and the Soul,* is convinced that human life can be fulfilled not only in creating and enjoying but in suffering. As he is a former inmate of Auschwitz and Dachau, we need not question his authority when he remarks that, 'to subtract trouble, death, fate and suffering from life would mean stripping life of its form and shape. Only under the hammer blows of fate in the white heat of suffering does life gain shape and form'. He also strongly asserts that it is not a doctor's province to sit in judgment on the value or lack of value of a human life. A physician's task, as assigned to him by society, is to alleviate pain and heal when he can, and nurse when an illness is beyond cure. How otherwise, he asks, would a patient differentiate between the doctor as helper or executioner? He argues that this principle admits of no exceptions. 'It applies', he says, 'to the incurable disease of the mind just as well as to incurable diseases of the body'.

Concerning those born mentally deficient, whom some might consider to be an economic burden on society and unproductive and parasitic, Frankl goes further than some Christian theologians in demanding their right to live. Frankl states that the life of such a person, if surrounded by loving relations and if he or she is the irreplaceable object of their love, has meaning though it be only passive. In this respect we recall the words of Teilhard de Chardin addressed to his sister, who had suffered a life-time of serious illness: 'Marguerite, my sister!' wrote de Chardin, 'While I — devoted to the positive forces of the universe was traversing continents

42

and oceans, passionately concerned to see all the colours and beauties of the earth, you were lying there, stretched out motionless, transforming in your innermost being the worst darkness of the world into light. In the sight of God, our Creator — tell me — which of us two had the better part?' (*Teilhard de Chardin. A Guide to his Thoughts*).

4. Care of the dying

In January 1971 a special panel appointed by the Board of Science and Education of the British Medical Association published a report entitled *The Problem of Euthanasia*. Briefly, and before considering the question of care of the dying, it is relevant at this point to consider just a few of the Report's more important findings.

In the section called 'Death', for example, the report says: 'The general public commonly suppose that dying is inevitably a difficult and distressing process. The fact that the majority of deaths are peaceful, whatever the preceding illness, needs greater emphasis. Contrary to popularly held opinion, even the majority of patients suffering from cancer die peacefully. It is in the preceding stages of terminal illness that relief of pain and distress is needed. Some of the emotion behind the demand for euthanasia lies in the belief that death will be peaceful and dignified only after a lethal injection'.

Later on it states under 'Medical Problems': 'Control of pain and alleviation of distress must be the object and not termination of life. Pain is relieved in other ways — by reassurance and by confidence and by rest. Doctors are assisted in this by nurses, by the professions ancillary to medicine and by ministers of religion. The sympathy and support of relatives and friends is also extremely valuable'.

43

Under the heading 'The Elderly', the report remarks that: 'The argument that the elderly are "kept alive by the use of drugs" has been grossly exaggerated. There is much evidence to show that even the most potent remedies may become relatively ineffective in old age. Old people are kept alive by kindness, good nutrition and good nursing . . . It would be primarily the distress of the relatives that would be relieved by euthanasia'.

In its sixth section, entitled 'The Medical and Nursing Profession' there is this statement: 'Those who support euthanasia have always assumed that doctors will both assess the patient's need for it and undertake the task. The decision whether or not to adopt euthanasia would be made, primarily, by society but society could not expect the medical profession to carry it out. To be a trusted physician is one thing; to appear as a potential executioner is quite another. If patients, particularly the elderly and those with cancer phobia, believed that doctors would play an active part in euthanasia some would fear their doctors and possibly avoid them, thereby failing to obtain essential and curative treatment'.

The report's final sentence is short and succinct: 'Killing patients is no part of the work of doctors and nurses'.

Even if the BMA Report had never been published, Christians would still have had the task of ensuring that care of the dying came high on their list of priorities. What else is the parable of the Good Samaritan about but loving others, whoever they may be and especially if they are in need? We are all familiar with Jesus's description of those meriting a place in his kingdom as those who feed the hungry, give drink to the thirsty, welcome strangers, clothe the naked and visit those who are sick or in prison (Mt. 25:31-46). We are also aware of his

44

injunction to 'be compassionate as your Father is compassionate. Do not judge, and you will not be judged yourselves; do not condemn, and you will not be condemned yourselves . . .' (Lk. 6:36-37). It is surely here that we find the appropriate rôle for ourselves in care of the dying?

Compassion is one of those words which one could spend a life-time unpacking, as it were, its various meanings. Any one tending someone dying may be called upon at different times to behave in a variety of ways, all of which eventually would come under the heading of compassion. Moreover, though it may be true that medical resources to alleviate pain are considerably more available today, such as in the skilled use of drugs, surgery, radiotherapy, the ability to delay the development of abnormal blood cells, and even the anaesthetizing of nerve fibres and thereby interrupting pain impulses from passing from a diseased area to specific parts of the brain, ultimately it is compassion for the person being tended that more often than not produces the most effective reduction of pain, agitation, anxiety and depression this is true of all our relationships with others, but even more so of our relationships with those who are dying.

In the first instance, compassion involves regarding sick persons as individuals, as important in themselves, and as unique people. R.D. Laing, the psychiatrist, illustrates this tellingly in the story he relates of an old lady who had spent many years in a mental hospital. One day a new nurse appeared on the old lady's ward. At tea time, (an event which had featured in the daily routine of the ward from time immemorial), the new nurse offered the old lady a cup of tea. The old lady said 'Thank you' and then, to the nurse's surprise, added: 'Do you know, this is the first time for years that anyone has actually *offered* me a cup of tea'. The old lady did not mean that she hadn't had a cup of tea for years. What she was implying was that for longer than she could remember her afternoon cup of tea had either been pushed in front of her, quickly handed to her, and hurriedly poured out as just one more cup on a loaded trolley passing by her. For years she had been drinking tea without, in a sense, being considered, and without her feelings being taken into account; she had been taken for granted, and disregarded as a human being made in God's image.

The trouble is that we are all so rushed, so busy and have so many things on our minds. As a Carthusian once remarked: 'Like bees our faculties come and go ceaselessly, settling and feeding upon any object that presents itself . . . These objects are good, but they are not the ultimate good. They are from God, but they are not God. He is the hive where the honey is made'.

What would have happened had Jesus been like so many of us in our dealings with others, instead of basing his conduct on his understanding of his Father's will discovered in prayer? Jesus had more than the knack of noticing people in a crowd such as Zaccheus in the sycamore tree; he also had compassion in the second sense of the word.

Confronted with the leper who approached him and who went down on his knees and sought healing, we are told that Jesus 'feeling sorry for him, stretched out his hand and *touched* him' (Mk 1:41). We can imagine the reaction of the onlookers. According to the law of the time, lepers were ordered to wear special clothing, to keep their hair disordered and to live apart from the rest of the community. At the approach of other people they were to declare themselves loudly and clearly 'unclean'.

It is perfectly clear from the gospels that Jesus was a person who took the sufferings of others seriously, who exposed himself to their needs, and who placed himself at the disposal of those in distress and trouble. Perhaps one of the most revealing instances of his compassion, best defined in modern terms as empathy, was shown in his reaction to the distress of Mary, the sister of Lazarus. When Mary threw herself at Jesus's feet declaring that if he had been present Lazarus would not have died, we are told that: 'At the sight of her tears, and those of the Jews who followed her, Jesus said in great distress, with a sigh that came straight from the heart, "Where have you put him?" They said, "Lord, come and see". Jesus wept; and the Jews said, "See how much he loved him!"' (Jn 11:33-36).

Compassion is respect for a terminally sick person as an individual, and empathy with his or her feelings and outlook thus enabling us to enter into his or her emotional reactions to situations including those of acute suffering. Compassion also has connotations of providing companionship. Affection, trust and sympathy are all ingredients of true companionship, but an equally essential element is a readiness to listen, implying a willingness to share. Paradoxically, those who have spent a great deal of time caring for the dying often record that what they have been called upon to share is not always anguish but at times joy. This comes out frequently in the writings of Dr Cicely Saunders, Medical Director of St Christopher's Hospice, and an authority on nursing those with a terminal illness: 'One of my greatest friends was a girl who was only forty years old when she died. For the first years I remember she gradually became paralyzed and blind and for the last three years was totally without sight and almost without any movement at all. Many of us came to be her friends, but it was another patient who best summed up what one saw in her as she lived on in the midst of this slow dying of her body. As she came away from her bedside one afternoon this patient said to us, "The incredible thing is, you don't even feel sorry for her: she is *so* alive". Her dying had become the very means of her growth, for we learnt from her husband that her intense aliveness, gaiety and interest in other people had developed during her illness. Always we remember her laughter, and more vivid by the occasional tears that showed us how much this cost her. The less her body could do the more her spirit shone, in love and amusement and a clear-sighted wisdom concerning life and those she met' (*Dimensions of Death. A talk originally commissioned by the BBC*).

It is incumbent therefore on any one tending the dying to try to be sensitive to, to understand, and to respond appropriately to the other's needs, whether they be physical, mental, emotional or spiritual. This often calls for personal sacrifice in the shape of time, energy and resources, but this is the thin line determining the difference between compassion and love. It is this line that Christians must cross in giving witness to the fact that euthanasia is not the answer to pain and suffering.

It was love for example which impelled Mother Teresa of Calcutta to take an old man found in a ditch into her now famous home for the dying. He was virtually a heap of bones enclosed in a thin parchment of crumpled skin but had just a glimmer of life left in him. Mother Teresa washed him and cared for him even though he was soon to die. Before he died, however, the old man muttered in Bengali: 'All my life I have lived like a beast, and now I am dying like a human being. Why is this?'

3
The Christian
attitude to suicide

For the greater part of her life Jane enjoyed all the material opportunities this life could give. She was a business woman by profession and highly successful. Regarded by her friends and acquaintances as a 'fun-loving person', she was well-known at parties and a popular figure in her local pub. Her great joy was her annual cruise to the Mediterranean.

In her late seventies Jane's business had to be sold, her husband died, and once her money dwindled Jane's good-time friends deserted her. She then lived alone surrounded by mementoes of the 'good days'. In time she became stone-deaf. On one occasion she fell and broke a hip, on another she broke the other. She became a prey to depression.

One morning the home-help found Jane dead in bed with a plastic bag over her head. Her funeral was pitifully sad. At the graveside were two distant relatives, one remaining friend and the home-help.

1. Past attitudes
The old man dying in Mother Teresa's care did not live long enough to receive a reply. Many people indeed might wonder why long before, given his situation, the

old man had not taken his own life as Jane did.

Until 1961, to try to commit suicide was a legal offence in Britain. Before then, as Professor Joad once remarked, you could not commit suicide without being regarded as a criminal if you failed and as a lunatic if you succeeded.

In the ancient world there was no one attitude to suicide. Greek philosophers such as Pythagoras who had an exalted view of the Absolute, or those such as Socrates and Plato who possessed an awareness of the unseen world, were opposed to suicide. Aristotle (384-322 BC), who subsequently was to have a profound influence on medieval theologians and Christian thinkers, considered suicide unethical. On the other hand, the Stoics, who came later, approved of it. It was their opinion that when a person was tired of life he was free to take his leave. Among other Greeks suicide was tolerated when it was occasioned by patriotism or a desire to avoid dishonour.

In Roman times more than a few were largely influenced in their view of suicide by such legislation as Justinian's *Digest* which declared that suicide was not punishable if occasioned by 'impatience of pain or sickness or by any other cause . . . by weariness of life . . . lunacy . . . or fear of dishonour'.

When we search the Old Testament for evidence and views of suicide we find that only four are actually recorded (those of Samson, Saul, Abimelech and Achitophel), and they are not particularly condemned. It is true, however, that after the exile in Babylon it was considered noble among the Jews to die for the faith, but even so tragic in other circumstances. In the first century AD suicide was strongly condemned by Josephus, the Jewish historian and soldier, even in times of war. His outlook probably reflects that of typical pious Jews

50

of his times, but they did not influence the Jewish Zealots besieged at Masada who in 73 AD preferred mass suicide to capture by the attacking Romans.

In the New Testament Judas Iscariot's suicide is simply stated without comment.

It would appear that what initially prompted the Church to legislate on the matter of suicide, and what made St Augustine in particular take an interest in the subject, was the rise of the Donatist heresy, the adherents of which may have sought 'premeditated martyrdom' to further their cause. When Donatists started hurling themselves off cliffs, Augustine defined suicide under any circumstances as 'a detestable and damnable wickedness'. He not only interpreted the sixth commandment to include self-killing, but taught that since life is a gift from God suicide is tantamount to rejection of God's gift. He also regarded it as an act of cowardice and a way of attempted escape.

From the early sixth century, therefore, we find various Councils of the Church legislating on the matter of suicide. In 533 AD the Council of Orleans denied funeral rites to anyone who killed himself while accused of a crime. Twenty-nine years later the Council of Braga denied funeral rites to all suicides, regardless of social position, cause or method. In 693 AD the Council of Toledo made even attempted suicide an excommunicable offence.

Catholic teaching on the subject of suicide was subsequently refined by St Thomas Aquinas. In his *Summa,* suicide is described as a mortal sin against God who has given life; it is also a sin against justice and charity. Made in God's image, man is not the author of his own life nor its absolute owner; suicide is a rejection of God's love and a denial of his sovereignty. Aquinas like Augustine before him also states that it is a violation of the sixth commandment, and regards it as an act of despair which precludes repentance.

After the Reformation, Protestants laid less emphasis in their teaching concerning suicide on the arguments of Augustine and Aquinas; they preferred to concentrate their arguments on the meaning of the sixth commandment alone. Even so, they were at one with Catholics in considering it a sin. Moreover, despite assaults against various Christian teachings from such philosophers as David Hume (1711-1776) during the eighteenth-century Enlightenment, the Christian view as it were held the field in the western world until the end of the nineteenth century.

2. Causes of suicide

With the publication in 1897 of Emile Durkheim's *Suicide: A Study in Sociology,* the consideration of suicide gradually shifted from the moral to the sociological point of view. Investigation of social conditions which it was thought might account for suicide became fashionable. From the 1920s onwards, other specialists ranging from statistical analysts and psychoanalysts to social workers, joined in the study of the subject. In 1953 the Samaritans came into being, as did similar organizations throughout the Commonwealth and the USA.

Durkheim classified suicides into three types: the egoistic, the altruistic and the anomic; each being the product of a specific social situation. The egoistic type of suicide occurred when an individual experienced a breakdown in the social structures or patterns to which he had been accustomed; the altruistic took place on behalf of a group with which the individual identified, such as Captain Oates' death on the Antarctic expedition; the anomic was the result of a traumatic experience, as for example a death in the family or the sudden loss of occupation. Durkheim concluded that the suicide rate increased in proportion to the rise of tension and unease in society.

Since Durkheim's investigations, others have either questioned or qualified his findings. Freud linked suicide with mourning and melancholia. He considered that a man might take his own life partly to atone for his fantasied guilt for the death of someone he loved. Other psychologists have noted how frequently persons who attempt suicide experienced the death of a parent when they were children. In recent times research has highlighted the occurrence of social isolation as a factor in suicide, and Erwin Stengel in his *Suicide and Attempted Suicide* has added enormously to our understanding of the problem and has destroyed a great many myths surrounding the subject.

Stengel has demonstrated for instance that it is untrue that those who threaten to commit suicide never do, and that those who have attempted suicide never try again. The poet Alvarez was writing from personal experience when he said: 'Suicide is like diving off a high board: the first time is the worst'. Stengel also suggests that the incidence of suicide rises with age, reaching its peak when people are between fifty five and sixty, with the young being the great attempters. All however are appealing for help, and seventy-five per cent of successful and would-be suicides give clear warning of their intentions. A curious discovery of Stengel's is the cycle of self-destruction: it precisely follows nature's seasons. Suicides decline in number in autumn, reach their low in mid-winter, rise slowly in spring, and attain their peak in early summer.

In the field of statistics, however, we can probably learn less about actual suicide rates than about the manner in which deaths are classified, so wide are the disparities throughout Europe in the means used by a coroner or his equivalent to reach a verdict. Nevertheless, according to a World Health Organization public health paper published in 1974, Hungary has the highest suicide rate for both men and women in Europe and Ireland and Malta the lowest. Finland, Austria, Czechoslovakia and Sweden follow closely on the heels of Hungary in respect to men; Denmark, the Federal Republic of Germany and Austria in regard to women.

Even so, given sociological, psychological and statistical knowledge together with the fact that much of it is open to question, one is still left with the question of what should be the attitude of Christians to suicide? Whatever the socio-medical evidence may add to our understanding, for a Christian suicide remains a moral issue.

3. The Christian approach

The removal of civil penalties for attempting suicide and the abolition in certain countries of such practices as penalties for the families of suicides are obviously civilized steps, but the treatment of suicide as merely a sociological phenomenon has bred a certain amount of public indifference to the subject. The penalties of the Church — when they were enacted — may have seemed harsh, but at least they did not suggest that suicide was something to be treated lightly. Their intention was preventative.

In today's world, it is estimated that at least a thousand people take their own lives each day. In Britain the figure is a hundred each week, as well as twenty-five to fifty others not officially designated as suicides. Somehow or

54

other the Church has to continue to express its concern about the gravity of such a situation in its teaching, and simultaneously combine modern insights into the subject with all the compassion it can muster.

Nevertheless, that brings us back to the question of how an individual should react if confronted with someone seriously contemplating suicide. What should influence what we might say and how we should behave as Christians towards such a person?

According to the Catholic psychiatrist Dr Jack Dominian: 'The determined attempt to end life arises from the conviction that life holds little prospect of any further value or significance.' He cites as examples which give rise to such a conviction: adolescents feeling trapped within the home with authoritarian parents; young people unable to reach a decision regarding their future or a personal relationship; broken engagements; the trapped spouse; the failed exam or business venture; public or private disgrace.

In the light of what Dominian tells us, surely a Christian should be in a position to throw light on the value or significance of the life of any human being he or she meets. Even Nietzsche once observed that 'Whoever has a reason for living endures almost any mode of life'. Our problem is more often than not the practical one of how to convince a would-be suicide that his or her life is of value. How does one for example reassure a young woman, whose boy friend wanted nothing more to do with her when she told him that she was pregnant, that life is still worth living? What should one say to the mother who took an overdose after her husband deserted her and their two children? How does one give hope to a middle-aged man whose wife and son have been killed in a road accident and who sees no point in life?

55

Initially, we again must adjust ourselves simply to listening to the other without betraying prejudice, shock, disgust or surprise. We must not only listen but show by our attitude that we care. To make appeals at this stage to the other person to pull himself or herself together, or even to 'preach', is usually counter-productive. Basically what is most needed is the ability to convey by our behaviour and manner, not so much by what we say, that he or she before us is valuable, irrespective of what he or she may have done or be contemplating doing. Inwardly, of course, simply listening can be exhausting, time-consuming and take much patience. These and other reactions are summed up by the poet Ian Caws in his poem *Suicide Threat:*

> I watched her, playing emotions like cards,
> Shuffling them in her mind. For a slow hour,
> I listened to her rattling life and death
> Like counters. Her vanity turned me sour,
> The making trivial of all meaning
> In her existence. Temper, sobby, breath,
>
> Pleas, threats, all in their turn. She was leaning
> Harder, threw in the children (who would find
> Her) like an extra stake. What is it kills
> Pity, that rubs out feelings which are kind?
> Sulky, she slammed the door on my harsh words.
> Upstairs, I knew, was the bottle of pills.

If, however, this art of listening is truly cultivated, and with prayer becomes more than mere politeness, then an aware Christian is enabled to move further in a relationship with the person experiencing distress. A few years ago a priest received a visit from a young woman sent to him by her social worker at the mental hospital where she was attending as an out-patient. This young woman saw no point in life, no point in living and, having been badly let down in the past, was now frightened to make relationships with others. The social worker thought the priest might be able to help this woman, provided he never mentioned religion or God, since the woman in question had made it clear that she intensely disliked both.

When the young woman arrived the priest encouraged her to talk about her past life, her relations with her parents, her former interests and in fact anything she chose. It was clear that she thought it strange at first to be talking to a priest, especially one who spoke very little except to ask an occasional question. For his part he deliberately and simply tried to put the young woman at her ease and to understand by listening what possibly lay beneath what she was actually saying.

To his surprise the young woman asked at the end of the meeting if she could come again; in fact she started coming regularly and always the meetings took the same pattern. Then one day quite unexpectedly she asked him if he ever got depressed and what sort of things made him ever unhappy.

Truthfully he had to say that what sometimes made him sad was the thought and sight of so many people today who apparently never give God any thought or time or room in their lives, who are indifferent to God's love and existence. He took the woman to the window of his room which looked down on the streets of a large city centre. 'We are all so busy', he said, and then pointed to people who could be seen hurrying everywhere. He pointed to women rushing by doing their afternoon shopping, to others running to catch buses, to young men roaring past on motor-cycles, to cars and lorries speeding down to the ferry or the docks, and to children rushing to get home from school. The whole scene resembled something out of a Lowry painting.

'How many of the people you see', the priest asked her, 'do you imagine have communicated with God their Creator today? How many of them have a personal relationship with Jesus and regard him as more important than any one or anything in their lives? For how many is Jesus as alive to them as the members of their families or people they are perhaps hurrying to meet?'

'Perhaps a few but not the majority', she replied.

After that the young woman didn't come to see the priest quite so often, but she started phoning regularly to say that she had begun to pray to God — the God whom the social worker had advised the priest never to mention.

Today that young woman spends almost all her free time visiting people who are lonely, especially the elderly and the isolated, such as Jane whom I mentioned at the beginning of this chapter. She herself has come alive to the meaning of St Paul's words, 'The life and death of each of us has its influence on others' (Rom.14:7). Moreover, because she has herself known suffering in the past, she is now able through the strength she derives from prayer to relate effectively with others; and through listening and empathy, she is able to shed light on the meaning to be found in the particular Gethsemanes of others. She knows their sorrows.

Since Jesus himself in the Garden of Gethsemane, faced with the injustice and cruelty of his situation, prayed: 'Father, if it is possible let this cup pass from me', we can all do the same. It is natural and absolutely right not to wish to be put too severely to the test. Even so, Jesus's words 'if it is possible' indicate that he did not regard God his Father as an escape hatch, someone

58

who would assist him evade all the horrors and hurt of suffering. He did not turn to his Father for a pain killer or relate with him as though he were a magician, someone to whom one could appeal to supply one with tranquillizers to alleviate doubts, fears, anxieties or pain. In other words Jesus did not confuse reality with escapism.

Humanly speaking, wasn't Jesus in Gethsemane, frightened and suffering from the feeling of being cornered? (St Mark's account states that Jesus was 'panic-stricken'). Isn't it also conceivable that he felt that his life's work had been a total failure? It was, after all, only after the resurrection that Jesus (in St Luke's version) was able to open his disciples' minds to understanding the fact that 'it is written that the Christ would suffer and on the third day rise from the dead'.

During those bleak hours before his arrest, when even his closest followers failed to stay awake and comfort him in his agony, Jesus experienced possibly the most cruel form of suffering, namely the feeling of having been rejected, misunderstood and abandoned.

Precisely in deciding not to evade his stripping, beatings, torture and crucifixion he achieved victory. Refusing to be mastered by his agony, he made it his servant instead.

Lest this should sound beyond the ability of the average man or woman, it is perhaps useful to reflect on the example of a woman who in contrast to Jane did not give way to despair.

Susan was a woman in her middle forties and renowned in the large comprehensive school, where she was employed as the head of her department, for her brilliance as a teacher and for her organizing ability. Her work in a sense was her life; the needs of her pupils came before all else. At the height of her powers Susan was suddenly and without warning laid low with cancer. For the next

59

eleven months she was in and out of hospital to receive treatment. Although she fully knew her illness was terminal she adamantly refused to delude herself that it was otherwise. Her constant outlook was expressed in the words: 'This is my state. This is the corner I'm in. This is reality'.

Ultimately the cancer even penetrated her bone structure and one witnessed in a sense the very disintegration of her body before one's eyes. The incredible thing was Susan's acceptance of what was happening to her; it brought her knowledge of a dimension of life unknown to most of us. For the first time in her life God became a reality to her. This kind of experience has been well described by Anthony Bloom: 'God helps us when there is no one else to help. God is there at the point of greatest tension, at the breaking point, at the centre of the storm. In a way despair is at the centre of things – if only we are prepared to go through it. We must be prepared for a period when God is not there for us and we must be aware of not trying to substitute a false God' (*School for Prayer*).

Those who visited Susan in hospital wondered at her ability to refuse to take her mind off her approaching death or narcotize her feelings; she regarded both things as not coming to terms with reality. Susan had somehow learnt that it is those whom he loves that God tests like gold in a furnace (Wis. 3:6). Like Jesus before her, Susan did not flee from her agony even mentally. She did not regard God as someone who would provide a formula for getting her out of her devastating situation.

We ourselves may never have to undergo physical suffering on this scale, but it is not beyond the bounds of possibility that we shall be faced with intolerable hurt in our lives. Someone we love may die or let us down. Our material circumstances may change unexpectedly. We may have made a wrong decision or pursued wrong paths in life and then become a prey to depression. Something we set our heart on achieving may not be realized or may even collapse. We may discover previously unknown and unpleasant sides in our make-up such as having a proneness to worry or a sense of failure ending in bitterness. Examples could be multiplied. Even so, apart from sin, there is nothing we have to face that in a sense Christ did not undergo when he was on earth: 'It was essential that he should in this way become completely like his brothers so that he could be a compassionate and trustworthy high priest of God's religion, able to atone for human sins. That is because he has himself been through temptation he is able to help others who are tempted' (Heb. 2:17-18).

Clearly this especially includes the temptation to despair which so often ends in suicide.

4
Love as the basis of hope

As a young child Stephen was sent to boarding school. It was the first time he had ever left home and the effect on him was frightening. Because it was his parents who had sent him away, he wrongly but understandably at the time interpreted their action as one of rejection. Furthermore, he came to believe that since his own parents did not love him he must in himself be somehow unlovable.

Throughout his teens and even when he came to enjoy and appreciate the benefits of life at boarding school, Stephen nevertheless unconsciously continued to believe that no one could ever possibly love him. He despised himself.

It was not until he was at university and when a comparative stranger once saved him from drowning that Stephen was able to acknowledge with his heart, as distinct from his head, that he was after all of value and capable of being loved. There was no other way to explain his rescuer's behaviour.

1. The place of renunciation
In his second letter to the people of Corinth, St Paul wrote: 'Though the outward part of our nature is being worn down, our inner life is refreshed from day to day'.

(2 Cor. 4:16). Contrary to possible first impressions, Paul is not here contrasting what was occurring to his body on the one hand to his spirit on the other. As St Augustine in the fifth century and Ladislaus Boros in our own have observed, basically Paul was alluding to the two processes through which a person's life on earth passes, one of which may replace the other the closer one draws to death.

The first process begins at conception. Thereafter the earthly life of each of us passes through different stages of being an ovum, an embryo, a baby, a child, an adolescent, a young adult, a middle-aged and then an old person. As is readily observable, this process resembles a steady growth from helpless dependence to apparent maturity and self-mastery and then gives places to an equally steady but relentless and irreversible decline to total dependence again.

For St Paul, this first process concerning 'the outward part of our nature' which in time is 'being worn down', has more to do with the claims of egoism and selfish ambition than with physical growth and decay. He was aware that when this first process is at its peak in maturity a person may be exercising talents associated with simply achieving wordly ambitions, power, position, possessions, success and even fame; his sensitivity to the existence of eternal realities may be blunted; even his expressions of love may be snares and delusion 'Even the saints', says Boros, 'have found that their love of their neighbour was constantly threatened with collapse, that it was not love that was given to them, but the obligation to love. Their constant lament is this: one begins to give oneself selflessly, tries to seek only the welfare of one's fellows, to help those who are in need, to comfort the afflicted, to live for another in love, and all at once one discovers

64

that in all this lay hidden dreadful falsehood, a hollow self-deception' (*The Moment of Truth*).

Even so, as Paul claimed for himself and as the example given by Dr Cicely Saunders earlier and quoted in the section 'Care of the dying' indicates, it is possible that the more the 'outward part of our nature' declines, the more our 'inner life' may grow. The 'inner life' mentioned by Paul as being 'refreshed from day to day' is a reference to discovering man more fully as valuable and as made in God's image and to acquiring a deeper awareness of the paramount claims of a dimension beyond the purely material and earthly.

Though it may be that the older (and, we hope more truly wise) we become, the less we put our faith and trust in ephemeral things, we cannot afford simply to wait for the 'outward part of our nature' to begin declining, and then automatically anticipate the growth of our 'inner life'. How a man chooses to live according to the 'outward part' of his nature frequently determines what happens to his 'inner life'. We are to a large degree the product of our choices, decisions and quality of our relationships. This is shown, for example, by the case of the man whose whole life was changed by an insight obtained in a sudden and dramatic way.

As a young man Jonathan was an infantry officer in the second World War. Wherever he went he carried with him a knapsack containing the material objects he most treasured in life, ranging from the pocket-watch given him by his mother, the first razor bought him by his father, his favourite book of poetry, and so on; they were all things he 'clung to' to remind him of home.

One day during an enemy artillery barrage a mortar shell landed on top of Jonathan's knapsack and totally destroyed everything he chiefly prized in life. At first he was stunned and shocked and the pain of his loss was almost physical, but quite suddenly he felt a wonderful inner freedom. Since then he has fought a relentless battle against ever again clinging to, or being possessed by, or even becoming attached to particular material possessions.

Jonathan's behaviour might strike some as extreme but it is only a reflection of the truth uttered by the un-canonized saint of Russia, John of Kronstadt: 'That to which a man turns, that which he loves — that he will find. If he loves earthly things, he will find earthly things, and these earthly things will abide in his heart, will communicate their own earthiness to him, and will find him; if he loves heavenly things, he will find heavenly things, and they will abide in his heart, and give him life . . .' (*My Life in Christ*).

No one knows how long his life on earth may be. We are all familiar with Jesus's parable of the rich man who planned to build bigger barns to house his bumper harvest and then spend years, so he thought, in self-indulgence, but who died that same night (Lk. 12:16-21). This parable was told by Jesus to illustrate a point he frequently made, namely: 'Watch, and be on your guard against avarice of any kind, for a man's life is not made secure by what he owns, even when he has more than he needs' (Lk. 12:15).

The true way of 'refreshing our inner life' from day to day can begin today, not necessarily when we are in the final stages of our earthly life. In addition it is the most effective means of countering egoism and all the delusions associated with self-seeking. It is the path of love along which Christ himself trod, and he is always there ahead of us beckoning.

The brief but traumatic episode of Stephen, mentioned at the head of this chapter, had all the qualities of a 'liberation'. Thereafter, because his rescuer from drowning had as it were 'emptied' himself of any concern for his own life, Stephen began to understand that genuine love necessarily entails renunciation. This enabled him much later to appreciate with sheer astonishment the extent of Jesus's love for us. 'Why else, except out of love, would the Son of God "empty" himself in the manner described by St Paul?' he used to ask. 'His state was divine, yet he did not cling to his equality with God but emptied himself to assume the condition of a slave, and became as men are; and being as all men are, he was humbler yet, even to accepting death, death on a cross' (Phil. 2:6-8).

Since Jesus had been prepared to go to these lengths, the young man, Stephen, saw no reason for not placing his faith in the promise of eternal life which Jesus made to his followers.

2. *Aspects of promise and salvation*

If we carefully examine the Scriptures, we find more often than not that eternal life is proffered in terms of promise of salvation, which in its essence is God himself. This comes across particularly in Jesus's use of the expression 'the kingdom of God'.

The 'kingdom of God' implies the notion of a God who acts, who has intervened in human history, and who is working with a dynamic and specific end or purpose in mind. In other words, it suggests an age to come when God's reign will be apparent. What so startled the Jews, however, was Jesus's declaration that, 'The appointed time has come. The kingdom of God has arrived' For those with faith the kingdom was present already in the person of Jesus himself and his ministry. 'The kingdom of God is in your midst', he taught (Lk. 17:21), and he added: 'Blessed are the eyes which see what you see. For I tell you that many prophets and kings desired to see what you see, and did not see it, and to hear and did not hear it' (Lk. 10:23-24).

When Jesus prayed 'Thy kingdom come', however, for him the kingdom was evidently that of his Father. In one sense, it had arrived with the incarnation and subsequent death and resurrection of Jesus; in another it was still in a process of growing, which was why Jesus laid the foundations of a new people of God, the Church, and at the Last Supper inaugurated a new covenant.

Eschatology, or the study of what theologically are termed the last things, is an aspect of a promise already given. As the Swiss Protestant theologian, Karl Barth, has observed, eschatology is not simply 'a harmless little final chapter'; its whole momentum is characterized less by prediction concerning when and how the kingdom will be fully and finally realized (1 Thess. 5:1-3; 2 Thess. 2:1-3), than by a promise requiring faith from us.

A promise of salvation eliciting faith from us might indeed be considered the hall-mark of God's dealings with mankind, whether we are thinking of the Old or of the New Testament (Heb. 11). Promises, however, are the product of personal relationships which are unpredictable. We have only to think of our own baptismal promises or of the promises made by a couple when they marry, those made by members of religious orders when they make their solemn profession, or those made when a man is ordained a priest. No one knows what the future holds for these relationships entered into; inevitably they will change and possibly develop and deepen; the only guarantees of their steadfastness are the faith, love and fidelity invested in the promises. From God we have a moving statement: 'Does a woman forget a baby at the

68

breast, or fail to cherish the son of her womb? Yet, even if these forget, I will never forget' (Is. 49:15).

When Jesus tells us 'I am with you always' (Mt. 28:20), and when in what is known as the high-priestly prayer he says, 'Eternal life is this: to know you, the only true God and Jesus Christ whom you have sent' (Jn 17:3), it is clear that what lies ahead for the person with faith is unending communion with Christ in his Father's house. In the meantime, we need to keep in mind the words of St John: 'My dear people, *we are already the children of God* but what we are to be in the future has not yet been revealed; all we know is, that when it is revealed we shall be like him because we shall see him as he really is' (1 Jn 3:2).

What is required of us as 'children of God' is to build and foster our relationship with God, just as in any personal relationship. This means that until the kingdom of God is finally realized we should be a people of hope, concerned with developing our faith in God by cultivating a continuous awareness of his presence in each moment of our lives, by giving time to prayer and to studying his word, and by meeting him in the sacraments. Equally, as so many of Jesus's parables are intended to show, membership of his Father's kingdom entails cultivating and practising love of others. As St Paul told the Corinthians; 'There are three things that last: faith, hope and love, and the greatest of these is love' (1 Cor. 13:13).

Those of us who are not in pain, distress or suffering must empty ourselves of self and place ourselves at the disposal of those who are and for whom love means surrender, especially the total surrender involved in death. The promise to which we must all cling, come what may, is that in the fully-realized kingdom God will wipe away all tears from our eyes and death shall be no more. Neither will there be mourning, crying or sorrow, for these will have passed away (Rev. 21:4).

3.   The life of love

We have seen that, according to St John, those who even now are 'the children of God' will ultimately become like God himself. In this connexion it is important to appreciate that in the same Epistle John defines God as love (1 Jn 4:8, 16). When he informs us that in the future we shall 'see' God as he really is, he means that we shall see that God's very essence is love. For most of us, this idea of our becoming like God and our seeing in the sense of assimilating love is extremely hard to grasp. We may be able to conceive such a possibility without being able to imagine it. Even the mystics throughout the ages have only been able to hint at what it means or use metaphors to describe it.

The process described by St John may be expressed as the full flowering of the seed implanted in every Christian at baptism. Moreover there are times in the lives of certain Christians when God permits them to experience and to glimpse as it were something of what St John tells us lies ahead of us after death.

This was certainly the case with St Augustine, as is evident from a passage in his *Confessions* describing an experience he shared with his mother, Monica, shortly before she died: 'Not long before the day on which she was to leave this life . . . My mother and I were alone, leaning from a window which overlooked the garden in the courtyard of the house where we were staying at Ostia . . . We were talking alone together and our conversation was serene and joyful. We had forgotten what we had left behind and were

70

intent on what lay before us. In the presence of Truth, which is yourself, we were wondering what the eternal life of the saints would be like, that life which no eye has seen, no ear has heard, no human heart conceived . . . Our conversation led us to the conclusion that no bodily pleasure, however great it might be and whatever earthly light might shed lustre upon it, was worthy of comparison, or of mention, beside the happiness of the life of the saints. *As the flame of love burned stronger in us and raised us higher towards the eternal God,* our thoughts ranged over the whole compass of material things in their various degrees, up to the heavens themselves . . . Higher still we climbed, thinking and speaking all the while in wonder at all that you have made. At length we came to our own souls and passed beyond them to that place of everlasting plenty, where you feed Israel for ever with the food of truth. There life is that Wisdom by which all these things that we know are made, all things that ever have been and all things that are yet to be. But that Wisdom is not made: it is as it has always been and as it will be for ever — or, rather, I should not say that it has been or will be, for it simply is, because eternity is not in the past or in the future. And while we spoke of the eternal Wisdom, longing for it and straining for it with all the strength of our hearts, for one fleeting instant we reached out and touched it. Then with a sigh, leaving our spiritual harvest bound to it, we returned to the sound of our own speech, in which each word has a beginning and an ending — far, far different from your Word, our Lord, who abides in himself for ever, yet never grows old and gives life to all things' (*Confessions.* Bk. IX, 10).

Augustine's account of his and Monica's mystical

experience is moving,* but we might be excused for thinking that since most of us are not of their calibre such experiences are beyond our ability. It would seem that the higher mystical states are attained by only very few Christians on earth. Moreover they are always a sheer gift of God. None of us, however, if Christian, can escape the commandments reiterated by Jesus himself that we should love God with all our heart, soul, mind and strength and our neighbour as ourself (Mk 12:30-31). Furthermore, unless we actually try to fulfil these commandments, how can we know that we shall never be granted a foretaste of what it means to become like God and to see Love in its very self? Fortunately, since 'we are already children of God', even now certain truths should be evident to Christians.

The first of these is that God loved us before we were able either to love him or anything else; without his love we should neither have existed in the first place nor continue to exist. Our very creation and continuous existence are acts of love, since God in himself lacks nothing. Included in our creation was one of the glories attached to being a human being, namely the gift of free-will. What would the world have been like without free-will? According to Gerald Vann: 'If none of his (God's) creatures had free-will, what a neat and tidy place the world would be: all things joining together in an unsullied song of praise to God; no problem of evil, no problem of pain, no problem of hell, no hatred. No hatred; but also

---

*For the person anxious to understand both the natural and Christian reactions to the death of a loved one, there is much he might learn from pondering upon Augustine's behaviour and attitude of mind on the death of his mother, Monica, as related in his *Confessions*.

no love, no friendship: and it was love and friendship that God wanted most of his creation; it was to make love possible that he gave some of his creatures freedom' (*The Seven Swords*).

Even now a Christian should be aware that love accounts for Jesus having come to earth and having been prepared to suffer, die and rise for mankind. Love motivated all that Jesus did for us and all that won man's redemption. 'God's love for us', wrote St John, 'was revealed when God sent into the world his only Son so that we could have life through him; this is the love I mean: not our love for God, but God's love for us when he sent his Son to be the sacrifice that takes our sins away' (1 Jn 4:9-10).

In an earlier section I spoke of the rôle of the Holy Spirit. We must ask ourselves if in our everyday lives we actively encourage and invite the Spirit of God to dwell within us. Is our intimacy with the Spirit of God such that we can describe the Holy Spirit in the manner of the fourteenth century Franciscan poet, Jacopone da Todi, when he says: 'Thou art the love with which the heart loves thee'? Do we find reality as well as beauty when Thomas Merton writes: 'To say that I am made in the image of God is to say that love is the reason for my existence; for God is love. Love is my true identity. Self-lessness is my true self. Love is my true character. Love is my name. I who am without love cannot become love unless Love identifies me with himself. But if he sends his own love, himself, to act and love in me and in all that I do, then I shall be transformed, I shall discover who I am and shall possess my true identity by losing myself in him. And that is what is called sanctity' (*Seeds of Contemplation*).

Certainly no Christian acquainted with the thought of

73

St John would question that he considers love of God and love of one's neighbour to be inseparably linked. 'My dear people', he writes, 'since God has loved us so much, we too should love one another' (1 Jn 4:11). In the case of someone who is troubled as to whether or not he or she is genuinely loving God, there may be real cause for doubt, but love of our neighbour cannot so easily be debated. This at least was the view of the formidable and yet so human Teresa of Avila who once remarked dryly: 'We cannot know whether we love God, although there may be strong reasons for thinking so, but there can be no doubt about whether we love our neighbour or no' (*The Interior Castle.* V, III, 8).

Our love of God is best fulfilled in attempting to do his will, not by worrying and fretting about our motivation — disinterested or not — or our emotional state at any given time. To someone experiencing distraction in prayer and not obtaining any emotional uplift, Dom John Chapman wrote: 'It is not necessary to want God and want nothing else. You only have to want to want God, and want to want nothing else. Few get beyond this really! But God is loving and takes not only the will for the deed but the will to will, or the wish to will' (*Spiritual Letters*). Moreover, the old saint who replied to the question whether it was easy or hard to love God by saying that 'It is easy to those who do it', was not simply being ironic. Time and again, as Newman observed, the saints have emphasized that if we wish to be perfect, we have nothing more to do than to perform the ordinary duties of the day well. We need to keep within the 'round of the day', as Newman says, or, as he wrote in his poem *Lead, Kindly Light;* 'I do not ask to see the distant scene — one step enough for me'. This is sufficient because 'we are already the children of God'.

And that is why uniting our will with that of God *now* should be our main preoccupation. If we succeed in this it is possible that we shall understand the nature of, for example, St Augustine's love of God, compared with which ours may at the moment seem tepid: 'What do I love when I love Thee? Not beauty of bodies, nor the fair harmony of time, nor the brightness of the light, so lovely to the eye, nor the soft melody of many songs, nor the sweet smell of flowers and ointments and spices, nor manna and honey, nor the limbs acceptable to embraces by the flesh. None of these I love when I love my God. Yet I love a kind of light and melody and fragrance, meat and embracement of my inner man: where there shineth unto my soul what space cannot contain, and there soundeth what time beareth not away, and there smelleth what breathing disperseth not, and there tasteth what eating diminisheth not, and there clingeth what satiety divorceth not. This is what I love when I love my God' (*Confessions.* X. 6).

At this point we may legitimately ask what all this talk of love has to do with pain, suffering, disease, depression, despair, loneliness, rejection and death. Are they not the very antithesis of love? The answer is that in heaven certainly they do not exist, but for those of us still on earth they are often mysteriously connected. The human heart is the symbol and central source of love; on earth suffering is often the other side of the coin known as love. It is no accident that among her remarkable spiritual experiences St Teresa of Avila included the mystical piercing of her heart by a spear of divine love. In a similar way, in 1544 St Philip Neri experienced an ecstasy of divine love which left a permanent physical effect on his heart. We should not be surprised, too, when we read of Simeon's prophecy to the Virgin Mary that,

immediately after uttering his memorable *Nunc Dimittis,*
he foretold the suffering in store for her and used the
symbol of a sword piercing her soul (Lk. 2:35).

In every type of pain and suffering there is the material
of self-offering, which is of the essence of genuine love,
as Christ himself showed us. Moreover, whatever crosses
we may be called upon to bear, in the last analysis there
is only one cross. 'To help other men, out of charity, is
to help God in his agony; to help God is to help the race
of men', remarks Gerald Vann. He adds that the smallest
action of this kind has a cosmic value.

It is the same therefore as love of God and love of our
neighbour. 'The love of me', Christ informed Catherine
of Siena, 'and the love of your neighbour are one and
the same thing, and to the extent that the soul loves me,
it loves him too, because its love towards him emanates
from me' (*Dialogue*). Furthermore, it is through prayer
that we attain to any real grasp of what lies ahead of us
after any pain and suffering: in other words, after death.
If we try to 'imagine' into the future, we are exercising
a faculty restricted to the material and sensible world.
In prayer, on the other hand, we are *willing* to be with
God and relate with him. There we receive a foretaste of
what we shall know fully after death, for we are already
children of God. In the meantime it is imperative to recall Christ's guarantee given at the Last Supper:

> I tell you most solemnly,
> you will be weeping and wailing
> while the world will rejoice;
> you will be sorrowful,
> but your sorrow will turn to joy.
> A woman in childbirth suffers,
> because her time has come;

but when she has given birth to the child she for-
   gets the suffering
in her joy that a man has been born into the world.
So it is with you: you are sad now,
but I shall see you again, and your hearts will be
   full of joy,
and that joy no one shall take from you.

(Jn 16:20-22).

Further reading (Part I)

Augustine, *Confessions* (Harmondsworth, 1961)
Anthony Bloom, *School of Prayer* (London, 1970)
Ladislaus Boros, *The Moment of Truth* (London, 1965)
Ladislaus Boros, *Pain and Providence* (London, 1966)
Ladislaus Boros, *Living in Hope* (London, 1969)
Ian Caws *Bruised Madonna* (London, 1979)
Dom John Chapman, *Spiritual Letters* (London, 1935)
Jack Dominian, *Depression* (London, 1976)
Geoffrey Gorer, *Death, Grief & Mourning* (London, 1972)
Michael Hollings & Etta Gullick, *The Shade of His Hand* (Great Wakering, 1973)
Michael Hollings, *I Will Be There* (Oxford, 1975)
Michael Hollings, *Alive to Death* (Great Wakering, 1976)
John Hinton, *Dying* (Harmondsworth, 1972)
C.S. Lewis, *The Problem of Pain* (London, 1960)
C.S. Lewis, *A Grief Observed* (London, 1961)
Louis Marteau, *Words of Counsel* (London, 1978)
E.L. Mascall, *Grace and Glory* (London, 1961)
Colin Murray-Parkes, *Bereavement* (Harmondsworth, 1976)
C. Saunders, *Care of the Dying* (London, 1960)
Erwin Stengel, *Suicide & Attempted Suicide* (Harmondsworth, 1973)
Hugh Trowell, *The Unfinished Debate on Euthanasia* (London, 1973)

Gerald Vann, *The Seven Swords* (London, 1952)
Gerald Vann, *Christian,* vol.2, no.4 (Eastertide, 1975)
Gerald Vann, *On Dying Well. An Anglican contribution
to the debate on euthanasia* (London, 1975)
Gerald Vann, *The Way,* vol.16, no.2 (April, 1976)

Part II
Made perfect
in weakness

1
The essence of sin

A form of blindness

As a child, long before the days of television, one of the most terrifying experiences I can remember was a dramatized radio version of H.G. Wells's story *The Country of the Blind*. As I recall, a traveller in a mountain region lost his way in a violent storm. Seeking shelter from the elements he stumbled into a valley not marked on any map. No sooner had he entered the valley than a landslide behind him cut off any possibility of retreat. He was then not merely lost but apparently trapped.

This was only the first of his trials; the worst was to come. It transpired that all the inhabitants of this unknown and mysterious valley were blind. Furthermore they thought that blindness was a normal condition; they had no idea what the traveller meant when he spoke of 'seeing' things. Their whole way of life was conditioned by their blindness. In this particular country it was the man who could see who was the odd man out. The people of this land concluded that he was mad.

Whether the traveller seeking shelter and becoming trapped in the country of the blind ever escaped I cannot remember. I do recall however how frightened I was when to normalize the man the residents of the valley decided to cut out his eyes and make him like the rest of them. I have never forgotten the story.

In the consumer societies of the western world it is not difficult to find parallels to the country of the blind. In our near idolization of wealth and the material possessions that money can buy; in the quest for power and sometimes the use of terrorist methods to obtain it; in the large-scale indifference to others' needs and suffering; in the endless pursuit of pleasure for its own sake; are we not in danger of becoming 'blind' without realizing it? And blind to the true meaning of life.

Christians would claim not to be blind. Even so, if we take our 'sight' for granted or refuse to try to enlighten the society in which we live, we are liable to fall victim to an even greater danger: namely, that of pharisaicism.

St Augustine was right when he remarked that a man who is illiterate can admire the beauty of script, the clearness and evenness of lettering, but cannot see the beauty in the meaning of what he reads. By analogy, many cannot perceive the dwelling of Christ in his servants and friends because they are without faith. Nevertheless, that does not excuse any of us from trying to indicate, to whomever we meet, and whatever our particular circumstances in life, that Jesus Christ is the one in whom the meaning of life is to be discovered.

This of course is made more difficult by the fact that for many of our contemporaries the Church as an institution has no relevance to their lives. Whatever other reasons may be advanced for this state of affairs, this indifference may be partly attributable to modern man's blindness to the meaning of sin. Over twenty years ago Pope Pius XII remarked: 'The greatest sin of our time is that it is losing the very concept of sin'. Pope Paul VI stressed that the need for renewing our sense of penance was 'among the grave and urgent problems of our time'.

A French author has gone so far as to maintain that the cleverest thing achieved by the father of all lies in our time is to convince us that he, the devil, no longer exists.

Strange though it may sound, however, the very existence of the Christian Church presupposes that sin does exist. If sin were imaginary, the Church and its message would be pointless. In the profoundest sense, the life, death and resurrection of Jesus can be understood only when set against the reality of sin.

Jesus did not come to earth and go around preaching, teaching and healing and ultimately rise from the dead simply to impress his disciples. His conquest of death in the resurrection was *the* sign that he had accomplished his essential mission on earth, and had overcome that which held mankind in thrall: namely, sin. The writers of the New Testament see it as an essential function of the Church to continue this mission of Christ and to free us, if we so choose, from sin's continuing stranglehold. This is what the good news is all about. This is the purpose of the sacraments; they enable us to participate in the new life won for us by Christ himself.

Even so, what is sin, why did man need to be 'rescued' from it by Christ and how does it still affect us?

Legalism versus the Spirit
Though few people nowadays are able to recite the Ten Commandments by heart, and possibly even fewer ever give them much thought, only a minority would not know what was referred to if they were mentioned. The drama of God handing the Commandments over to Moses on Mount Sinai is a story which seized the minds of many of us when we were children. It has frequently touched the imagination of film producers. What a

85

writer once described as God's gift of these 'great guns to a primitive people' is well-known.

At the time of Christ, though the Commandments remained, the Jews could no longer be described as primitive; they were highly civilized. Even so, they were strangely different from other peoples. For example, they showed no interest whatsoever in art, science or jurisprudence for their own sake. Their concern in politics was motivated by a desire to be rid of the Romans occupying their land. Yet they were indisputably a people of immense vitality, moral energy and keen intelligence.

Historians accounting for this state of affairs usually point to one obsessive concern of the Jews — their devotion to the Law and the Promise. The Law by now however meant not only the Ten Commandments. These by the time of Christ resembled an immense coral reef in the sense that over them had grown a vast series of crustations: artificially-preserved rules, regulations and requirements governing every aspect of daily life. Altogether the Law contained 365 prohibitions, 278 positive requirements and endless deductions casuistically interpreted and elaborated. A model pious Jew was aware, even though he might not understand their purpose, of a multitude of rules covering a variety of things from ritual and ceremony, sacrifices, cleanliness and uncleanness, marriage, and dietary laws, down to dead bodies and particularly the Sabbath. The point of the Law was to secure obedience. It was this that was thought vital; it was considered that which would secure for the Jews the Promise: namely, that Yahweh would be their God as opposed to all others.

Though Jesus was adamant that he had come not to destroy the Law and the Prophets, but to fulfil them

(Mt. 5:17), it requires very little imagination to understand his often expressed impatience with those pharisees who insisted to the point of pedantry on the maintenance of the Law. At one point Jesus denounced them as 'straining over gnats and swallowing camels' (Mt. 23:24) and at another he quoted Isaiah: 'This people honours me with their lips but their heart is far from me. They worship me in vain with their teaching of the precepts of men' (Mk 7:6-7).

In a similar way it is arguable that for too long sin has been interpreted by Christians too much, and sometimes solely, in terms of a failure to obey specific laws, either of God or the Church. Disobedience either in the form of doing something forbidden or of not doing something commanded us has often been the *only* way in which we have viewed sin. This has been well described by the moral theologian, Charles Curran: 'Too often sin has been considered only in terms of the model of law and obedience which emphasizes sin as a specific external action. These actions were then thoroughly categorized and catalogued in lists. Sin as an external action viewed in the light of obedience to the law of God is a very inadequate model for understanding the reality of sin. A mechanical individualistic, and actualistic concept of sin robbed sin of its real existential meaning for the Christian. Perhaps it is true that the world has lost the sense of sin, but even more unfortunate is the fact that Catholic Christians have lost a true understanding of sin' (*Contemporary Problems in Moral Theology*).

In the New Testament the most commonly used word for sin is *harmatia,* derived from the notion of shooting, and meaning a missing of the target. Sin is a failure to hit the target; it is falling short of the mark. Curran sees sin as that which destroys relationships with God, between man and man, and between man and creation. In other words, sin or the failure to hit the target is rooted in what he calls 'the refusal of man to accept the gift of God's love'. Without this love man cannot love God, his neighbour or himself: this is the fact that is of paramount importance.

When we fail to take account of God's existence, and ignore or take for granted the love shown us by Christ; when we fail to love or even consider the needs of our fellow men and women; when we fail in our responsibilities as parents or as off-spring; when we fail to use and employ the talents God has given us or think only of ourselves; whenever we fall short of the best we can be, then we sin.

How sin entered the world

This failure on the part of man and the entry of sin into the world have been brilliantly described in the third chapter of the Book of Genesis. The insight into the nature of sin found in this reflective meditation squares with the idea of sin as essentially that which destroys relationships. Though a particular act of disobedience is described in the chapter, the motive behind it implied a love of self rather than of God; a refusal to trust in God's love: 'The serpent said to the woman, "You will not die. For God knows that when you eat of it (the fruit of the tree in the midst of the garden) your eyes will be opened *and you will be like God* . . ."' (Gen. 3:4-5).

It was this desire to be like God, to put his own interests first, and to give way to the temptation proposed, which undermined man's relationship with God. Afterwards, Adam and Eve hid themselves from God; they no longer enjoyed their previous loving relationship with him, described in terms of walking with God in the cool of the day (Gen. 3:8).

As a result of their alienation from God (the author of life), death inevitably entered the world. A further major consequence was the disruption of the hitherto loving relationship between man and woman. After the original refusal to abide in God's love, Adam was fully prepared to place the blame on Eve (Gen. 3:12), whom until then he had rejoiced in as 'bone of his bones and flesh of his flesh'.

Before the Fall Adam had also been depicted as king of all creation; he had been given the right of naming all the animals, which was a momentous act implying that Adam had a say in the particular character each animal henceforth possessed. After sinning this harmonious relationship between man and creation was broken. From then on Adam and his descendants were to know suffering, sweat, fatigue and labour. Eve would experience the pains of child-birth.

For many people the Genesis account of how sin entered the world is no longer tenable; it is rejected almost immediately as clearly outmoded and too much like a fairy story to have any bearing on life in the twentieth century. To dismiss it thus, however, is to miss the point and to fail to penetrate beneath the surface language of the story to the reality of its message. Equally, it is dangerous to reject the account as childish.

In *Voyage to Venus,* a science-fiction work in which C.S. Lewis penetrates remarkably to the inner meaning of the Garden of Eden, he describes the profound folly we so often commit: namely, in believing that temptations to sin must be sophisticated. The devil is capable of using any device to disrupt a loving relationship between man and God, and man and his neighbour. During the long and gruelling session in *Voyage to Venus* when the devil, possessed of the body of a physicist called Weston, is tempting the Lady of Venus, the hero of the book, Ransom, has ample opportunity to observe this: 'Ransom had full opportunity to learn the falsity of the maxim that the Prince of Darkness is a gentleman. Again and again he felt that a suave and subtle Mephistopheles with red cloak and rapier and a feather in his cap, or even a sombre tragic Satan out of *Paradise Lost,* would have been a welcome release from the thing he was actually doomed to watch. It was not like dealing with a wicked politician at all: it was much more like being set to guard an imbecile or a monkey or a very naughty child . . . It showed plenty of subtlety and intelligence when talking to the Lady; but Ransom soon perceived that it regarded intelligence simply and solely as a weapon, which it had no more wish to employ in its off-duty hours than a soldier has to do bayonet practice when he is on leave. Thought was for it a device necessary to certain ends, but thought in itself did not interest it. It assumed reasons as externally and inorganically as it had assumed Weston's body. The moment the Lady was out of sight it seemed to relapse . . . With Ransom himself it had innumerable games to play. It had a whole repertory of obscenities to perform with its own − or rather with Weston's − body: and the mere silliness of them was almost worse than the dirtiness'.

Another important aspect of sin delineated in Genesis is that what is forbidden very quickly appears all the more attractive, precisely because it is forbidden. This tendency was later high-lighted by Augustine: for example, in his *Confessions* when he writes of an occasion in his youth when he stole some pears. He had no need of them; he stole only to enjoy the theft itself and the sin. His real pleasure, he says, consisted in doing something that was forbidden.

Furthermore, as the Genesis account of how sin entered the world informs us, sin begets sin. No sooner had Cain become angry with his brother Abel than further sin was — in the eloquent wording of the text — to be found 'crouching at the door'; Cain conceived the idea of killing Abel. It is an almost universal phenomenon that once we have broken a relationship of love by an act of selfishness, we see little point in refraining from further similar, if not worse, acts.

Seeing beyond the rules
More important by far, however, than excessive concern for rules and regulations *per se* is the need to ponder their purpose. Obviously law as such is a necessary and natural dimension of any form of life, but when over-emphasized in regard to human beings and categorized in minute detail concerning our every action, it may quickly degenerate into something which produces only mechanical behaviour based on fear. It may also generate irrational scruples. We must be alive to both tendencies. We have seen how prevalent they were among the Jews at the time of Christ. Somehow, like the young author of the poem *I Hate Rules*, we must cultivate the art of seeing beyond the rules.

> Why do I feel so sick inside,
> so mad at myself?
> And why do I want
> to take out my feelings
> on someone or something?
> Why am I so confused
> about what is right and what is wrong?

God, If my parents knew
some of the things that go on in my head
I think they'd disown me.

They taught me the rules!
Don't steal! Don't swear!
Don't answer back! Don't be rude!

And every time I break the rules
I sin, they say!
I am guilty!
I am wrong!
I am bad!

But sometimes I'm not so sure
about the rules
or my parents
or the Church . . .
or being born
or me!

I hate rules
because, well, because they are just rules.
They are like squares on the floor,
like the circles of a target
at the rifle range,
like the lines running down the highway!

What if those targets were really faces?
And what if those lines were really lives?
And what if those rules were really people?

Then sin would be breaking people,
instead of breaking rules.
Sin would mean breaking up with God,
instead of breaking his laws.
Sin would be personal

and cruel
and wrong . . .

(*For Mature Adults Only,* N.C. Habel)

A lack of love
The young person above has concluded that sin results in alienation from God, from others and from one's authentic self. What has here been discovered instinctively was set down in formal terms centuries ago by such intellectual giants as Augustine and Thomas Aquinas.

Following Augustine, Aquinas for example defines evil as 'the absence of the good which is natural and due to a thing' (*Summa* pt.1 Q. XLIX, art.1). Deafness, for instance, is the absence of a good that is proper to a human being but not proper to a material object. Thought of in this way, moral evil at least exists only as deafness exists. It is not something additional, a substance or entity in itself, but an absence or lack of something good, of something which ought naturally to exist. When we fail to love God, our neighbour or ourselves (love in this context meaning willing good), we sin. This absence of love is at the root of moral evil. John says: 'If we say we have no sin we deceive ourselves' (1 Jn 1:8).

Is there anyone who at some time has not taken God for granted; failed to thank him for life, love, the faith, creation and so on; ignored him and failed to relate with him in prayer? Is there anyone who has not failed in charity, if only in his thoughts, concerning his neighbour? And how often do we let ourselves down by being lazy, lying, swearing, boasting, stealing, harbouring impure thoughts and so on?

Obviously there are degrees in our lack of love, hence the terms 'mortal' and 'venial' sin. A conscious decision to get drunk at a party and then to drive home afterwards, regardless of how much this might endanger others' lives, is clearly of a different order from being impatient with an elderly person who cannot move as quickly as in former times. Both however are instances of failure to love; both indicate a lack of consideration for others. It is as Jeremy Taylor said: 'No sin is small. No grain of sand is small in the mechanism of a watch'.

Since sin may be described as either a lack of or a refusal to love, it is small wonder that, when God's plan of salvation for mankind culminated in the incarnation of his Son, the latter should have stressed that the first commandment was that man should love God with all his heart, soul and mind and that the second commandment was to love his neighbour as himself (Mk 12:29-31).

What particularly saddened Jesus when he returned to his home village of Nazareth was the hardness of the people's hearts; for similar reasons he wept over Jerusalem. Rejection of an offer of love, or in other words a refusal to relate, can often be heart-breaking. In a sense rank hostility is easier to bear than indifference. At least this would seem to be the feeling expressed by the author of the Book of Revelation when he writes: 'I know your works, says God. You are neither cold nor hot! So because you are lukewarm, and neither cold nor hot, I will spew you out of my mouth' (Rev. 3:16). This lukewarmness is especially to be guarded against; it is often summed up as 'I couldn't care less'. Such an attitude ultimately results in our becoming what a student has described as the 'nothing people':

> The nothing people,
> they do not lie,
> they just neglect to tell the truth.

94

They do not take;
they simply cannot bring themselves to give.

They do not steal;
they scrounge.

They will not rock the boat;
but did you ever see them pull an oar?

They'll not pull you down;
they'll simply let you pull them up,
and let that pull you down.

They do not hurt you;
they merely will not help you.

They do not hate you;
they merely cannot love you.

They'll not burn you;
they'll only fiddle while you burn.

They are the nothing people;
the sins of omission people.

They're neither good nor bad
— and therefore worse.

(Anon)

Conversion or change of heart
According to Martin Luther: 'The ultimate proof of the
sinner is that he does not know his own sin'. This may
be the state of the 'nothing people'; the kind of people
so vividly described in C.S. Lewis's *The Great Divorce*
and depicted as souls from hell who on the whole decline
a proffered invitation to enter heaven.

As we become oblivious to our own sin, it is not

unusual for us to try and rationalize it. We are not slow to attribute much of our behaviour and attitudes to such factors as heredity, our social environment, the type of education we received when young, and the kind of up-bringing we received from our parents. Clearly these do have an influence on us, as do particular instincts, drives and needs that we may have; not to mention intelligence and personal talents, or their absence. Even when all these factors have been taken into account, however, a Christian believes that he has a real measure of free will. Moreover all of us, whatever our background, status, race or class, although made in the image of God, have at some time misused this free will and have sinned to a greater or lesser degree. It is part of our faith that baptized Christians, cleansed from original sin, are still capable of sinning.

The only exception (apart from Christ himself) who has not sinned or failed to love in the above-mentioned way was Mary, the mother of Jesus. This was not through her own merit but through the merits of her Son. Un-doubtedly tempted, as was Christ himself, only Mary never refused to love God or failed to will what was good for her neighbour or herself. It was hardly surprising that her cousin Elizabeth was able to greet her with the cry: 'Blessed are you among women . . .' (Lk. 1:42).

Since we are sinners it should be clear that we need to be 'rescued'. Our situation would be nothing short of intolerable had not Christ come into the world to do that. True and marvellous though it is that his coming was the culmination of a plan of salvation inaugurated by God almost from the moment that man first sinned (a plan wonderfully made plain in God's successive dealings with the people of Israel as recounted in the Old Testament), the important point is that we are no longer a people without hope. As Paul told his disciple Timothy: 'Here is a saying that you can rely on and nobody should doubt: that Christ Jesus came into the world to save sinners' (1 Tim. 1:15).

This is the good news that Jesus proclaimed. For our part, what is required is an assent to the message and person of Christ and a response in the form of repentance. 'The time has come', said Jesus, 'and the Kingdom of God is close at hand. Repent, and believe the good news' (Mk 1:15).

In this context repentance means conversion or a change of heart, from the Greek *metanoia*. Of himself and unaided, man is unable to achieve this; it is always the result of God's mercy and forgiveness. According to Thomas Merton: 'The soul of man, left to its own natural level, is a potentially lucid crystal left in darkness. It is perfect in its own nature, but lacks something that it can only receive from outside and above itself. When the light shines in it, it becomes in a manner transformed into light and seems to lose its nature in the splendour of a higher nature, the nature of the light that is in it. So the natural goodness of man, his capacity of love which must always be in some sense selfish if it remains in the natural order, becomes transfigured and transformed when the love of God shines in it' (*Elected Silence*).

Conversion or change of heart in the Christian sense is therefore a joyful experience, akin to that felt so keenly by the prodigal son on his return. Whatever form it takes, it involves awakening to the delusion of sin, responding to the call of Christ and, through grace, being given the ability to be reconciled to God. For some it is their first encounter with Christ; with most of us it is a form of homecoming after varying periods of tedious wandering.

The history of Christianity is littered with examples

of men and women who have in different ways, some dramatic and others the reverse, undergone conversion to the good news. In the New Testament one thinks of Mary Magdalen, the Ethiopian eunuch, the centurion Cornelius and Paul. Paul's conversion on the road to Damascus has inspired countless artists and writers down the centuries.

Another memorable convert was Augustine. After years of self-indulgence, dabbling in heresy and promiscuous living, he underwent a personal crisis which he later described as the light of salvation being poured into his heart. The crisis was resolved and Augustine was changed when his eyes fell on the verse from Paul's Letter to the Romans: 'Let us conduct ourselves as in the day, not in revelling and drunkenness, not in debauchery and licentiousness, not in quarrelling and jealousy. But put on the Lord Jesus Christ, and make no provision for the flesh, to gratify its desires'.

Others who experienced conversion in one way or another are the worldly chancellor Thomas Becket, the once frivolous Francis of Assisi, the ambitious soldier Ignatius of Loyola, the slave trader John Newton, the sixteen-year-old John Henry Newman and, closer to our own times, the writer and Cistercian monk, Thomas Merton. The latter describes well the spiritual odyssey his self-will imposed on him before he accepted Christ: 'God in his mercy was permitting me to fly as far as I could from his love but at the same time preparing to confront me in the bottom of the abyss, when I thought I had gone farthest away from him . . . For in my greatest misery he would shed, into my soul, enough light to see how miserable I was, and to admit that it was my own fault and my own work. And always I was to be punished for my sins by my sins themselves, and to realize, at least obscurely, that I was being so punished, and burn in the flames of my own hell, and rot in the hell of my own corrupt will until I was forced at last, by my own misery, to give up my own will' (*Elected Silence*).

When a conversion is genuine, it necessarily affects not only the individual and his relationship with God but his relations with his neighbour. A disciple of Christ is enjoined not to offer his gift at the altar if he is in conflict with his brother. Before doing so he must be reconciled with his brother. Similarly a Christian is expected to forgive his neighbour in the same way that God extends mercy. This is not only a requirement found in Jesus' parable of the debtor who failed to forgive a fellow servant (Mt. 18:23-35), but one embedded in the Lord's Prayer: 'Forgive us our trespasses as we forgive those who trespass against us'.

For a Catholic, conversion — whether dramatic or quiet — is only the beginning of a process which continues for the remainder of his earthly life. Joyful though it is, conversion is only the start. This has been amply demonstrated in the case of Augustine by one of his biographers: 'Though Augustine was finally converted and was never again to lose his faith in God, the furious rages remained, providing the ground-swell to the music he played for the rest of his life. He had loved "the perishable beauty of the body, the brightness of the light, the soft melody of the *cantilenae,* the delicious scent of flowers and the limbs made for the embracing of the flesh." His hot African blood was not stilled by the conversion: like many others he would have to wait until he was old before the fleshly demon was silenced: his senses remained keen, and the texture of his prose, urgent and demanding, mirrors his sensuality as it mirrors his violence. He was the least calm of the saints, the most impetuous, and even after his conversion he was able to talk about doubts as though he understood the matter well enough . . . Yet he was sustained by the vision in the garden, the momentary brightness. What had he seen? He can only hint at it. There was a sense of blinding, tumultuous peace, of dedication, of superhuman relief, even of superhuman grace . . .' (*The Fathers of the Western Church*, R. Payne).

It was to continue the work begun in conversion that Christ instituted the sacrament of penance or reconciliation, commonly referred to as confession. To experience a change of heart, to be reconciled to God and then to remain in Christ, was what Paul sought most for instance of the people of Corinth (2 Cor. 5:17-21). It was for the task of reconciling, healing the rifts occasioned by sin, that after his resurrection Christ gave his apostles the authority to forgive men their sins: 'Jesus said to them again, "Peace be with you. As the Father has sent me, even so I send you". And when he had said this, he breathed on them, and said to them, "Receive the Holy Spirit. If you forgive the sins of any, they are forgiven; if you retain the sins of any, they are retained" ' (Jn 20:21-23).

2

The sacrament
of reconciliation

A sacrament of joy
If we are honest I think most of us would admit that
we do not frequent the sacrament of reconciliation,
commonly called confession, as often as we used to.
Furthermore, unless we are exceptional, confession is
not something we like.

We may pray these days just as much if not more,
regularly attend mass and receive Holy Communion and
be more keenly aware of our duties in other ways as
Catholic Christians, such as having a need to be concerned
for the poor and the under-privileged, but when it comes
to confession we have dropped away.

The reasons for this are many, and some of them will
be dealt with later on, but what is perhaps really lacking
in much of our approach to confession is an ability to
see it as a sacrament of joy.

For too long we have associated going to confession
simply with drawing up an account of our weaknesses and
failings, which is not an exercise guaranteed to make us
feel happy or something to look forward to. The time is
long overdue when we need to view confession not only as
this, but as something within the framework of the whole
purpose of Jesus' birth, death and resurrection. In other
words, as a vital element of the Gospel or good news

conveyed by Jesus Christ, whereby man is reconciled to God and his neighbour and rendered at peace with himself; the antithesis of anything to do with anxiety and gloom.

Recently changes have encouraged us to take a fresh look at the sacrament of reconciliation. The insertion into the sacrament of readings from Scripture and the greater opportunities given us to open our hearts and minds to the priest hearing our confession (thereby increasing the likelihood of his understanding us better before he bestows on us God's forgiveness), are intended to enable us to find the sacrament more meaningful. Even so, many still hold back. Why is this?

In addition to the many and various reasons we give ourselves, could it be that we have lost that eagerness shown for example by Zaccheus when, given the opportunity and despite his shortcomings, he scrambled down the sycamore tree and — according to the text — 'joyfully' welcomed Jesus into his life? Have we forgotten that after Zaccheus' change of heart Jesus was able to say: 'Today salvation has come to this house . . . for the Son of Man has come to seek out and save what was lost' (Lk. 19:10).

On another occasion, when his friendship with supposedly dubious characters was questioned, Jesus turned on his critics. He made the purpose of his life's work abundantly clear when he said: 'Go and learn the meaning of the words: What I want is mercy, not sacrifice. And indeed I did not come to call the virtuous but sinners' (Mt. 9:13).

Even a cursory reading of the New Testament shows that Jesus did not remain content with preaching the need for a change of heart. Similarly, he did not associate with obvious sinners primarily in order to expose the latent self-righteousness in the religious leaders of the time. What scandalized the pharisees most and what should cause us to leap for joy was that Jesus exercised the power of forgiving sins; something which no prophet, including John the Baptist, had done.

This comes across most poignantly in the story in which Jesus is invited to a meal at the house of one of the pharisees, and a woman arrives 'who had a bad name in the town'. It requires little imagination to consider the effect she had on the company when she wept, wiped her tears from Jesus' feet with her hair, and anointed his feet with oil. Jesus did not use this episode simply to draw a contrast between the extent of the love shown to him by the pharisee and the woman; he went on to say to her: 'Your sins are forgiven' (Lk. 7:49).

Jesus continues to exercise this power today through the ministry of the Church and in the form of a sacrament. But how many of us take his words seriously: 'There is more *joy* in heaven over one sinner who repents, than over ninety-nine just who have no need of repentance' (Lk. 15:7).

In the parables of Jesus the recovery of a lost sheep or a treasured coin is an occasion for rejoicing (Lk. 15); so is the sacrament of reconciliation.

Obstacles in the way
In addition to this fundamental failure on our part to regard the sacrament as an occasion of joy, there are other factors which can stop our going to confession as much as in former times.

We may be frightened or dislike it. Who, after all, likes admitting that he has done wrong? Apologizing and feeling genuinely sorry are not enjoyable experiences, nor things that we find easy to do; they require courage. Even with friends and especially within our own family

103

we do not find it always a simple matter to admit that we are wrong.

But pride may be at the root of this fear or hostility. We wish to go on believing, or to have the priests who know us well believe, that somehow we are different from the rest of mankind. We may because of this deliberately avoid confessing to priests who might recognize us:

The Lord said,
'Say, We';
But I shook my head,
Hid my hands tight behind my back, and said,
Stubbornly,
'I'.

The Lord said,
'Say, We';
But I looked upon them, grimy and all awry.
Myself in all those twisted shapes? Ah, no!
Distastefully I turned my head away,
Persisting,
'They'.

The Lord said,
'Say, We';
And I
Richer by a hoard
Of years
And tears,
Looked in their eyes and formed the heavy word
Then bent my neck and lowered my head:
Like a shamed schoolboy then I mumbled low,
'We,
Lord'.

(Karle Wilson Baker in *Listen to Love*)

We may have become discouraged by the fact that whenever we went to confession in the past we always seemed to confess the same things. Only for a brief while afterwards did we seem to improve.

Finally the whole thing had become either rather mechanical and routine, or something which caused us too much worry. On the one hand, we may have resented as a child being pressed to go to confession by well-meaning parents, teachers or priests. On the other hand, we may have suffered too much from the harrassed feelings we had after doing something wrong, and from never feeling 'right with God' again until we had been to confession and had done our penance. Later on, neither confession as mere routine nor going because we somehow *felt* bad seemed adequate reasons for continuing.

Many of these attitudes were highlighted not so long ago in the book *Confession: Outmoded Sacrament?* by Sister Lawrence Murray. This book contained the results of a questionnaire the author had sent out to sixteen-year-old girls, all school-leavers, to discover what they understood by, and to what extent they were influenced by, the sacrament of reconciliation. The anonymous replies came from girls in industrial cities, the countryside, by the sea, in London, in a new town and in an old university city. Sister Murray extended her inquiries to Scotland, the United States of America and Basutoland. The number of girls who responded amounted to 1789. Despite the great differences in backgrounds, common features emerged from the answers.

Many girls expressed a definite need for help. As one English girl said: 'I worry about confession more than anything else'. Another remarked: 'I feel that confession should be something more. There seems to be no real contact between priest and the penitent. You go in and confess your sins mechanically, the priest sits and listens and gives your penance mechanically. I do not know what it is that is lacking, I have absolutely no idea, but I hope what I have said, though not very much has helped a little to find out . . .'

Opinions were divided on the question of whether they liked going to confession. Those who said No described confession as 'meaningless', 'inauthentic', 'just routine and done in parrot fashion', or they complained that they were 'treated as robots' or 'made to feel hypocrites'.

More than a few found it more frightening to tell a priest when they had last been to confession than to state their sins. On the other hand, they suggested that more emphasis was often placed on the telling of sins than on contrition and conversion. This inevitably meant, as one girl put it: 'When I go to confession, I am always more concerned trying to remember sins rather than thinking about the actual pardon'. Another admitted to feeling compelled to invent sins! 'I usually spend five minutes', she wrote, 'trying to think up some sins to tell the priest'.

Significantly and sadly, as Sister Lawrence pointed out, it was clear that most of the girls did not see confession as a meeting with Christ. The person of Christ indeed was rarely mentioned in the answers; much more frequent were such words as 'problem', 'embarrassed', 'communication', and 'scared'. Could it be that Sister Lawrence had put her finger precisely on what afflicts so many of us? It is possible that the girls who answered her questionnaire instinctively isolated why many of us go less often to the sacrament of reconciliation.

It might also be argued that nowadays we are all to some extent influenced by the materialistic and permissive society in which we live, or that by not going to confession so regularly we have over-reacted against the 'legalism' mentioned earlier.

For adults, a major obstacle is that many of them have rarely studied the purpose of the sacrament since they left school. This usually means that their understanding of it has not developed. They may be excellent parents and hold responsible positions at work, but when it comes to going to confession they revert to the language and thought-patterns of their late teens.

While realizing that the way they approach confession and speak to the priest in the sacrament are no longer appropriate to their age, they feel helpless or ashamed about this. This often applies to their whole attitude to religion and is typified by William Rees-Mogg, the editor of *The Times,* who in *An Humbler Heaven* writes: 'By the time I was thirty I still had the religion of a child, without benefit of the child's innocence and simplicity. I certainly did not give religion the attention I gave to the ordinary worldly matters with which I was dealing: I would have thought it shameful to know as little about economics or politics or literature as I knew about religion'.

The very least thing adults who experience problems in relation to confession might do is to revise their 'examination of conscience' before the sacrament, and to try to make it more relevant to their age and circumstances.

Whatever our age, we are possibly afraid of the demands unselfishness would make upon us. We have an uneasy feeling that Jesus' words, 'If anyone wants to be a follower of mine, let him renounce himself and take up his cross and follow me' (Mk 8:34-35), were meant to be taken seriously and, if put into effect, would require more than a slight upheaval in the life-styles of many of us. We prefer to sympathize more with Augustine's prayer before his conversion: 'Lord, make me chaste, but not yet'.

107

The rôle of the priest in confession

It has to be admitted that a few of us have sometimes been put off by the manner of the priest in confession. Instead of concentrating on the fact that we were there because we were sorry and sought to receive God's forgiveness, we failed to make allowance for the priest's own human failings. We may have stopped going to confession because the priest expressed impatience with us, was short or gruff in manner, and so on. We confused God's mercy and love with his human minister.

The new rite of penance should have clarified the priest's rôle in the sacrament. It should have helped to resolve many of the difficulties mentioned above. But obstacles take time to remove. In the meantime, therefore, we must remind ourselves that the priest in confession is the one who should help us to understand our relationship with God and our neighbour. He is also there to help us to be our authentic or real selves, freed from self-deceptions.

We also have to stop comparing the priest in confession to a judge in a court of criminal law. The latter often finds it necessary to know every minute detail concerning the case before him. He has the authority, if necessary, to demand the reconstruction of the crime alleged to have been committed by the person standing in the dock. His immunity allows him to make personal remarks about the accused, often of a scathing nature. If that is how we regard the priest hearing our confession, it is natural that we should be worried and even scared.

Nor should we liken the priest to a psychiatrist. Whereas a priest may act in an apparently similar way to a psychiatrist, if we visit him outside the sacrament of reconciliation and tell him our worries and problems, even then the situation is fundamentally different. It is not the function of the priest nor part of his training (unless he is specially commissioned) to be concerned in the first instance with our psychological state. Emotional hang-ups, complexes, phobias, inhibitions and even urges, drives and tendencies are not his prime concern.

Basically, the priest — whatever his personal skills and degree of perception — is ordained to preach the good news and to administer the sacraments. In confession he is the one who in God's name and through the ministry of the Church conveys to us God's forgiveness. His function is therefore to be an instrument reconciling a penitent with God and with other men and women. Like his Master before him, he is there to heal, to bind up wounds, and to convey peace.

Insofar as it is necessary for the priest to have a complete picture of the things we confess, this is solely to enable him to tell whether we are genuinely trying to reach out to God in sorrow. We need to confess as fully as possible because the priest's major task is to gauge the extent of our need of God's forgiveness and mercy, and the sacramental presence of Christ in our lives.

This man of flesh and blood
In 1941 a prisoner escaped from the notorious Nazi concentration camp of Auschwitz. As a reprisal the camp authorities decreed that ten men must die. They were to be starved to death in the dreaded, windowless underground bunker.

The prisoners were paraded in the blazing midday sun and ten victims were selected at random. One of them, Franciszek Gajowniczek, cried out in despairing tones: 'My wife, my children, I shall never see them again'. Then to the astonishment of guards and prisoners alike, a man stepped forward and offered to take Gajowniczek's place. He was prisoner 16670, Maximilian Kolbe, a Franciscan priest. 'Who are you?' asked the SS man in charge. 'I am a Catholic priest', replied Kolbe.

Throughout the next two weeks in the bunker, whenever the cells were opened the prisoners inside cried loudly and begged for bread and water, which they were denied. Father Kolbe neither begged nor complained but tried instead to raise the spirits of his fellow prisoners and to lead them in prayer. Eventually only four prisoners, including Father Kolbe, remained alive and the SS brought in a criminal who gave each of the four an injection of carbolic acid in a vein of the left hand. Praying as he did so, Father Kolbe offered his arm to the executioner. His death, declared another prisoner, was 'a shock filled with hope, bringing new life filled with strength . . . It was like a powerful shaft of light in the darkness of the camp'.

At a press conference following Father Kolbe's beatification in 1971, Cardinal Wojtyla of Cracow, now Pope John Paul II, emphasized that when Father Kolbe had been asked by the SS officer in Auschwitz who he was, he had replied, 'I am a Catholic priest'. 'So it was as a Catholic priest', said Cardinal Wojtyla, 'that he accompanied his wretched flock of nine men condemned to death. It was not a question of saving the life of the tenth man — he wanted to help those nine to die. From the moment that the dreadful door clanged shut on the condemned men, he took charge of them, and not just them but others who were dying of hunger in cells nearby, and whose demented cries caused anyone who approached to shudder . . . It is a fact that from the moment Father Kolbe came into their midst, those wretched people felt a protective presence, and suddenly their cells, in which they awaited the ghastly final dénouement, resounded with hymns and prayers. The SS themselves were astounded: *"So was haben wir nie gesehen"* (we never saw anything like it before), they said . . .'

At a time when so many priests all over the world are fretting about their 'identity', Father Maximilian Kolbe gives the answer, not with theological argument, but with his own life and death. He wished, like his Master, to prove that 'greater love hath no man than this . . .' – the ultimate test for a follower of Christ. We cannot all be heroes, but is it not a sign of failure if we simply refuse to be tested? . . .

'Father Maximilian died in an age of fury and contempt, in which men were reduced to the level of robots, lower even than slaves . . . Against that background only hatred can flourish . . . But the astonishing thing to which innumerable witnesses testify is that Maximilian Kolbe knew nothing of hatred. He looked at executioners and victims alike with the same clear gaze, to the point where even the most sadistic turned away, saying, "Do not look at us like that". This man, who was branded with the number 16670, won that most difficult of victories, *that of love which absolves as it forgives* . . .

'It is, therefore, no chance, but a sign of the times, that this priest who died in 1941 at the age of forty-seven in a famine-hole at Auschwitz should today be pronounced "Blessed", during this Synod which has as its aim the definition of the priestly ministry. To all the more or less abstract questions which have been asked, here is one concrete answer, this man of flesh and blood who carried out his commitment to the end . . .'

Confession of devotion

It may be that we already appreciate the rôle of the priest and recognize the value of the sacrament of reconciliation, but that our problem concerning confession is of a different kind. We may have convinced ourselves that on the whole our failings are really rather trivial, so we ask ourselves why we should go to the trouble of confessing them to a priest? We already know that deep down we are often immediately sorry for our unkind thoughts, our occasional swearing, our lack of patience, our half-truths, our lazy moments, and so on. Aren't these and things like them all rather paltry compared with the horrific acts we read so much about in our daily newspapers or see reported in the news on television? Of course Auschwitz was an abomination and Father Kolbe's priestly action heroic, but these are surely light-years away from my shouting at the children when they get boisterous, my annoyance with others when stuck in a traffic jam, my forgetting my night prayers, and so on?

It is when we start asking questions like these that we probably need to look again at the whole matter of what is traditionally known as the confession of devotion. When we find ourselves complacently reassuring ourselves that in any case we frequently acknowledge our unworthiness at the beginning of mass and at other points of the eucharist, but especially before actually receiving Holy Communion, perhaps we should think again.

It is interesting to note incidentally that these kinds of question and attitude are not new. Employing the familiar distinction between mortal and venial sin, both Thomas Aquinas and the Council of Trent addressed themselves to this state of affairs.

St Thomas maintained that the eucharist in particular was a remedy for venial sin. Christ, he says, had given a

112

means of taking away original sin in baptism, the personal grave guilt of mortal sin in the sacrament of penance and venial sin in the eucharist (*ST* III, q.75, a 2-4). This doctrine is found too in the deliberations of the thirteenth Session of the Council of Trent where it is stated that the eucharist is the antidote which frees us from daily sin (*DS* 1638).

Small wonder then that we ask what is the purpose of confessing our minor failings if we are regularly attending mass. And why should we bother to make only what is termed therefore a confession of devotion?

Sometimes it is argued that regular confession, even of sins which we might consider trivial and which are remitted in Holy Communion, enables us to know ourselves better. We do this by being assisted to open our hearts and minds to a confessor and receive from him spiritual direction that allows us to grow in faith and in our love of God and our neighbour. True though this may be, it is equally arguable that spiritual direction as distinct from counsel is best given outside the actual sacrament.

Another reason sometimes advanced for frequenting the sacrament of reconciliation regularly, even though we may have nothing serious to confess, is that it has what might be termed medicinal value. Good habits are established, weak inclinations are eliminated or controlled, and virtues are strengthened. Again this is true, but the decisive reason for going to confession no matter how insignificant our sins may seem, or in other words for the continuance of the confession of devotion, is of a different order.

Each of the sacraments may be said to have a specific purpose. So while it is true that in the eucharist we may obtain the forgiveness of our daily sins, this is not its chief end. In the case of the sacrament of reconciliation, on the other hand, the forgiveness of sins is its main and essential purpose. In going to confession, therefore, we are deliberately and consciously recognizing our sinfulness and the fact that all holiness and justice are derived from God not ourselves. In seeking God's forgiveness, even for minor failings, we are acknowledging that we are his creatures. We become aware, as was the poet George Herbert, of our proneness to sin, in spite of good intentions:

> Lord, with what care hast thou begirt us round!
> Parents first season us: then schoolmasters
> Deliver us to laws; they send us bound
> To rules of reason, holy messengers,
>
> Pulpits and sundayes, sorrow dogging sinne,
> Afflictions sorted, anguish of all sizes,
> Fine nets and stratagems to catch us in,
> Bibles laid open, millions of surprises,
>
> Blessings beforehand, tyes of gratefulnesse,
> The sound of glorie ringing in our eares:
> Without, our shame; within our consciences;
> Angels and grace, eternall hopes and fears.
>
> Yet all these fences and their whole aray
> One cunning bosome-sinne blows quite away.

Like most things we gradually give up doing, after the first few occasions we can in time produce any number of apparent reasons for no longer bothering. Whatever made us stop going to confession in the first place, for example, it is not difficult by now to have found countless other supposed reasons for not returning to the sacrament. Either we search our minds for more and more explanations to justify our behaviour, or we invent excuses, forgetting William James' dictum that, 'For him who confesses, shams are over and realities begin'.

This is especially so if what made us stop going to confession in the beginning was a personal moral issue; something which we wanted to do but with which we considered the Church did not agree. We then convinced ourselves that to continue going to confession would be hypocritical. In considering that our behaviour might be at odds with the Church's thinking, however, we have unwittingly stumbled on a vital truth; we have unconsciously recognized the social nature of sin and that — as we discussed earlier — it destroys relationships.

Members of one body
Whereas the sacrament of reconciliation has always existed in the Church from the time of the apostles, the form it has taken has changed immensely through the ages. In the early Church there existed numerous rites of penance and differing views concerning the gravity of specific sins.

Nevertheless the Fathers of the early Church agreed that, in addition to others, such sins as apostasy, murder, adultery and theft on a grand scale were always grave. The reason was that they damaged the community, the Body of Christ, the Church.

For that reason grave sins could only be forgiven through the community with the bishop at its head. In other words, since the result of the sin committed had inflicted harm on the community, genuine sorrow required the repairing of the damage done.

Usually, despite variations from place to place, the rite of penance in the early centuries consisted of three

115

distinct parts: the admission of guilt, the period of satisfaction, and reconciliation. And clearly the social nature
of grave sin was more obvious in the form that the sacrament took than in the private confession we know today.

Whereas a sinner was required firstly to make known
the nature of his sin to his bishop in private, or to the
priest to whom this task had been delegated, the actual
making of satisfaction and being reconciled were public.

The sinner was declared an official penitent and Lent
was usually regarded as the appropriate time for his per-
formance of penance. On Ash Wednesday, therefore, he
was clothed in sack-cloth, ashes were sprinkled on his
head which had been newly shaven, prayers were offered
on his behalf and he was then expelled from the Church
until Maundy Thursday. On Sundays throughout Lent
the sinner was obliged to stand outside the door of the
Church and beg the incoming worshippers for prayers.
This was in addition to his maintaining a strict régime
of fasting, abstaining from meat, and not participating
in public entertainments.

On Maundy Thursday the whole Christian community
would assemble with the penitent awaiting at the door
of the Church. At a particular point in the ceremony the
penitent would be permitted to enter and have the
bishop's hands placed on his head, thus bringing him the
forgiveness for which he had striven and prayed. At
mass he was once again permitted to receive Holy
Communion as a sign that the rupture he had occasioned
in the community had been healed.

Nevertheless heavy penalties remained on the forgiven
sinner for the remainder of his life. He was not permitted
to hold a post in the army, participate in business or
politics, become ordained or marry. Even heavier was
the fact that a sinner could only receive the sacrament

of penance or reconciliation once in his life-time. For obvious reasons, therefore, many Christians preferred to be reconciled only on their death beds.

It is small wonder too that at the beginning of the ninth century, when enormous liturgical reforms took place following the disruption of society in the Dark Ages, people were reluctant to see the former system of penance re-introduced. By then the practice of private confession had been brought to Europe by Celtic and Anglo-Saxon missionary monks such as Boniface. Reconciliation preceded satisfaction and, more important, the sacrament could be received as often as one wished. Furthermore, there were no additional penalties lasting a life-time.

Severely though the sacrament of reconciliation or penance may have been administered in the early Church, it did make plain that grave sin was never without social effects. As the French theologian Henri de Lubac explains: 'The efficacy of Penance is explained like that of Baptism, for the relationship is quite as clear, in the case of the former, between sacramental forgiveness and the social reintegration of the sinner. The double functions of this sacrament as a disciplinary institution and as a means of inner purification are not merely associated in fact; they are united, if one may put it so, by the nature of things. The Church's primitive discipline portrayed this relationship in a more striking manner. The whole apparatus of public penance and pardon made it clear that the reconciliation of the sinner is in the first place a reconciliation with the Church, this latter constituting an efficacious sign of reconciliation with God . . . In St Cyprian's view, for instance, the priest's intervention has for its immediate effect this "return" of the sinner, this return of one who has been "cut off"

117

(excommunicated) to the assembly of the faithful; the cleansing of the soul is a natural consequence of this re-immersion in the stream of grace, and it should be defined as a return to the "communion" of saints' (*The Sacraments as Instruments of Unity*).

Heavily influenced by an atmosphere of dominant individualism, all too often we have tended to think of our spiritual lives in relation to God, and have lost sight of the corporate effects of sin. We need a wider form of reference. It is to be hoped that the new rite of reconciliation will enable us to return to a deeper grasp of Christ's commandment: 'Thou shalt love thy neighbour as thyself'.

'This is not merely a helpful suggestion', says Thomas Merton, 'it is the fundamental law of human existence. It forms part of the first and greatest commandment, and flows from the obligation to love God with all our heart and soul and strength . . .

'Man is divided against himself and against God by his own selfishness, which divides him against his brother. This division cannot be healed by a love that places itself only on one side of the rift. Love must reach over to both sides and draw them together. We cannot love ourselves unless we love others, and we cannot love others unless we love ourselves. But a selfish love of ourselves makes us incapable of loving others. The difficulty of this commandment lies in the paradox that it would have us love ourselves unselfishly, because even our love of ourselves is something we owe to others' (*No Man Is An Island*).

Not long ago this social dimension of our faith was brought home to a priest when on his day off he went to visit a friend who was off work and recovering from pneumonia. In the afternoon his friend's wife arrived back for tea from a shopping expedition, accompanied by their three children, the eldest of whom was six.

Anyone with small children knows how chaotic and noisy meals can be and this one was no exception. At six o'clock, however, without any prompting, each of the children drifted off to get washed and ready for bed. Then the children summoned parents and priest to an attic bedroom.

There a candle was lit and anyone watching would have observed three adults and three children kneeling or squatting on the floor, and each of them in turn saying prayers not only for themselves but for people in need. This is a ritual for the parents and their children in that home. It takes place every night and the participants are quite devoid of self-consciousness.

That may not sound unusual, but in the flickering glow of that candle the priest felt himself a privileged guest. He also became aware that in that tiny attic room a tremendous power for good was being generated. He understood in a moving way the meaning of Jesus' words, 'Where two or three are gathered together in my name there am I in the midst of them'. He became aware of his own unworthiness in the company of this family and he understood more fully what Jesus must have meant when he said: 'I bless you Father . . . for hiding these things from the learned and the clever and revealing them to little children'.

That family together with the priest in that attic were a microcosm of the Church. But just as their concern for God and one another vividly communicated itself, so assuredly would any lack of love or sinfulness have affected all present. If we are weak or lukewarm in our commitment as members of the People of God, then the Church's ability to be the salt of the earth and a light in the world (Mt. 5:13-16) is inevitably less. If this is the case, then it is the sacrament of reconciliation which may bind up that which is broken or damaged not only between ourselves and God, but with all the people of God who make up the Church.

3
The Christian
meaning of conscience

It is axiomatic that unless the Gospel is preached and heard an individual cannot be expected to respond to it in faith. 'Faith', Paul told the Romans, 'comes from what is preached and what is preached comes from the word of Christ' (Rom. 10:17). It was for this reason that he enjoined his disciple Timothy to make preaching of the good news his life's work (2 Tim. 4:5).

It is probable that all of us, including those of us who would claim already to be Christian, need provoking as it were into appreciating our need for conversion or change of heart. On the other hand, few of us take kindly to being provoked to consider our failings.

The manner in which the people of Israel treated the prophets is by now proverbial, but the reason why prophets are still unpopular is not hard to understand. As someone said recently: 'A prophet is always a person who is a nuisance to other people, because he brings them face to face with themselves. He puts a mirror in front of their faces and they don't like what they see and that's why they get so angry'. To prevent ourselves getting angry, we have only to embark on our own examination of conscience. Moreover, if we fail to do this from time to time, it is unlikely that we shall ever fully grasp the meaning of sin, understand our need for reconciliation, or appreciate as mature Christians the true nature of the work of Christ. Our problem is compounded however by the fact that considerable confusion exists among Christians as to what is meant by conscience.

For a Christian 'freedom of conscience' does not mean enjoyment of the supposed prerogative to do, think, and speak whatever he pleases. 'To consider persons and events and situations only in the light of their effect upon myself', says Thomas Merton, 'is to live on the doorstep of hell. Selfishness is doomed to frustration, centred as it is upon a lie . . . When I give myself what I conceive to be freedom, I deceive myself and find that I am the prisoner of my own blindness, and selfishness and insufficiency' (*No Man Is An Island*).

Freedom of conscience is not a license to behave however a person may like or feel, provided that it would appear not to harm anyone else. For a Christian this would mean denying what was mentioned earlier, that we are members of one body; when a Christian advocates the rights of conscience he is not campaigning to be accountable for his views and conduct to himself alone.

Finally, a Christian does not confuse conscience with duty defined as what is useful, expedient, practical, or what seems best for the majority. Equally he rejects any theory suggesting it is something one is born with in the sense of a baby possessing innate moral ideas, a creation of man or of civilization, or merely the product of unconscious activity stemming from instinct. In one way or another the views of such people as Kant, Nietzsche and Freud when they allude to conscience are found to be wanting, if not totally unacceptable. So what does a Christian mean by conscience?

In 'A Letter to the Duke of Norfolk' in *Certain Difficulties Felt by Anglicans in Catholic Teaching,* published in 1876, John Henry Newman defined conscience as understood not only by Catholics but by Anglicans and Protestants. It would be enlightening however to discover how many of us have given the matter deep consideration; more than a few of us have probably unwittingly imbibed the vague notions held by the majority of our contemporaries. So often we confuse 'consciousness' with conscience. Certainly in the former we become aware of our emotions, our thoughts, desires and imaginings, and an examination of our consciousness is from time to time of value, but that is not what is meant by an examination of conscience. The latter is to do not only with ourselves but with God: 'I say', wrote Newman, 'that the Supreme Being is of a certain character which, expressed in human language, we call ethical. He has the attributes of justice, truth, wisdom, sanctity, benevolence, and mercy, as eternal characteristics in His nature, the very Law of His being, identical with Himself; and next, when He became Creator, He implanted this law, which is Himself, in the intelligence of all his rational creatures. The Divine law, then, is the rule of ethical truth, the standard of right and wrong, a sovereign, irreversible, absolute authority in the presence of men and angels. "The eternal law", says St Augustine, "is the Divine Reason or Will of God, commanding the observance, forbidding the disturbance, of the natural order of things". "The natural law", say St Thomas, "is an impression of the Divine Light in us, a participation of the eternal law in the rational creature". *This law, as apprehended in the minds of individual men, is called "conscience"*; and though it may suffer refraction in passing into the intellectual medium of each, it is not therefore so affected as to lose its character of being the Divine Law, but still has, as such, the prerogative of commanding

123

obedience. "The Divine Law", says Cardinal Gousset, "is the supreme rule of actions; our thoughts, desires, words, acts, all that man is, is subject to the domain of the law of God; *and this law is the rule of our conduct by means of our conscience".* Hence it is never lawful to go against our conscience; as the fourth Lateran Council says, Whatever is done contrary to one's conscience leads to eternal damnation'.

Clearly this view of conscience is, as Newman observed of his times, very different to that widespread in society today. It is no longer fashionable to believe that conscience is the voice of God nor as Newman went on to say, 'a messenger from Him who, both in nature and in grace, speaks to us behind a veil, and teaches and rules us by His representatives'. As in Newman's day, 'The idea, the presence, of a moral governor is far away from the use of it (the word conscience), frequent and emphatic as that use of it is. When men advocate the rights of conscience, they in no sense mean the rights of the Creator, nor the duty to Him, in thought and deed, of the creature; but the right of thinking, speaking, writing, and acting according to their judgment or their humour, without any thought of God at all'.

Many of the so-called definitions or usages of the term conscience prevalent today remain in fact what Newman called 'miserable counterfeits' of the real thing. Even so, it remains true as he further observed, that: 'the sense of right and wrong, which is the first element of religion, is so delicate, so fitful, so easily puzzled, obscured, perverted, so subtle in its argumentative methods, so impressible by education, so biased by pride and passion, so unsteady in its course that, in the struggle for existence amid the various exercises and triumphs of the human intellect, this sense is at once the highest of all teachers, yet the least luminous . . .'

It is utterly possible, then, for the Christian to have a conscience which is uninformed, immature or, as is said, simply bad. His conscience is rendered mature on the other hand in the first instance by the teaching and example of his parents. Later, at school for example, by the encouragement to adhere to the natural law, to study and reflect upon revelation as found in sacred Scripture and tradition, to understand the purpose of obedience to the teachings of God and the Church, and to practise the faith daily in prayer and the sacraments, bearing fruit in love of God and his neighbour. But how many of us ever achieve such spiritual adulthood?

Only in the lives of the saints do we find that, after a certain point, all external laws and teachings have been in a sense so interiorized and assimilated that the phrase of Augustine 'Love and do as you will' has meaning. The majority of us however will in some respects possibly always remain spiritually infantile, and therefore need props to support us; props in the form of laws or teaching designed to enable us to listen more effectively to that inner voice called conscience. In the Old Testament the word sometimes employed for conscience is heart. It was no accident, given his profound understanding of the importance of listening to the word of God, that Newman should have chosen as his motto, *Cor ad cor loquitur* (heart speaks to heart).

The most vital aid to the formation of one's conscience will always remain prayer. Thomas Merton indeed goes so far as to say that 'the whole function of the life of prayer is . . . to enlighten and strengthen our conscience so that it not only knows and perceives the outward, written precepts of the moral and divine laws, but above all lives God's law in concrete reality by perfect and continual union with His will' (*No Man Is An Island*).

In sending instructions to his disciple Timothy, Paul told him 'to fight like a good soldier with faith and a good conscience for your weapons' (1 Tim. 1:19). This remains the universal mission and armoury of every Christian in order that we may convey to others how Christ gives us both freedom and the forgiveness of our sins:

> As he is the Beginning,
> he was first to be born from the dead,
> so that he should be first in every way;
> because God wanted all perfection
> to be found in him
> and all things to be reconciled through him and for
>   him,
> everything in heaven and everything on earth,
> when he made peace
> by his death on the cross.
>
> (Col. 1:18-20)

4

The place
of the cross

Hardness of heart
Without a lively and informed conscience, it is impossible
to appreciate our need of forgiveness. Just as at the
very outset I suggested that a form of blindness prevents
many of us from understanding the nature of sin, so a
dull conscience will hinder us from approaching the
sacrament of penance. Related to both these forms of
spiritual deprivation, however, is an even greater danger:
namely, that of indulging in self-righteousness or of
harbouring a 'hardness of heart'. This is worse because it
impedes us from obtaining any insight into precisely
how Jesus 'made peace by his death on the cross'. Without such insight we almost inevitably fail to comprehend
the benefits of reconciliation; we may be oblivious to
the value and effects of forgiveness. In that respect the
parable of the prodigal son has much to teach us.

Throughout the great parable of the prodigal son it is
an interesting fact that the word 'prodigal' is never once
mentioned; it is we who have imposed the word on the
story. Moreover, because the parable is so obviously useful for inducing feelings of contrition, it has not been
unknown for preachers, for example, to concentrate on
that most spectacular sinner, the younger son, and ignore
the elder son completely.

Some people today prefer to call the story the parable of the forgiving father or, as A.M. Hunter calls it, the parable of the waiting father. Certainly few of us are not moved when we read how, 'While he (the younger son) was still a long way off, his father saw him and was moved to pity. He ran to the boy, clasped him in his arms and kissed him tenderly' (Lk. 15:20-21). That indeed may be how God is but how many earthly fathers would behave like that towards a son who had 'squandered his money on a life of debauchery'? The title parable of the forgiving father then is perhaps only slightly better than the parable of the prodigal son.

No matter what we call it however, it will doubtless continue to inspire painters, musicians and writers for many years to come, just as it has already exercised the imaginations of such diverse creative people as Rembrandt, Debussy, Prokofiev and John Masefield among others. It will also continue to fascinate theologians as they ponder on the precise symbolic meaning behind such things as the father giving a robe, ring and sandals to the son on his return, and as they dwell on the horror for Jesus' audience of the fact that the young man had been employed to feed pigs (unclean animals to Jews) when he had spent all his money 'in that distant country'.

But in our marvelling at the sheer beauty of the story we may miss the very point that Jesus is trying to hammer home: namely, that most of us are neither like the younger son nor the father but the elder son.

More than a few of Jesus' parables are constructed according to a precise pattern of rules. One might be based on what is known as the rule of contrast, in which virtue is contrasted with vice, riches with poverty, or wisdom with folly. Another might follow the rule whereby it contains three people, such as in the parable of the good Samaritan in which there are three travellers, the parable of the great banquet in which there are three excuse makers, and so on. But, especially in the parable known as that of the prodigal son, there is the rule in which the spotlight falls on the last person mentioned in the story. It is the elder son in this story on whom the emphasis should fall.

If one asks why, the answer is that it is because Jesus was telling the story to the scribes and pharisees; people known to be God-fearing, law-abiding and critical of Jesus' attitude towards sinners, but above all self-righteous or hard of heart. In the parable it is they who most resembled the elder son, and aren't many of us Christians like that? We are often blind to the truth contained in the words 'None are so far from God as the self-righteous'. We are adept at not seeing or hearing what we don't want to see or hear — particularly about ourselves.

Yet in the parable, and in his mercy, the father loved both his sons. It would be comforting if we knew that the elder son also eventually came to see the folly of his outlook and conduct. In our case certainly, it is only when we discover our own failings that we usually most often become aware in faith of how much God our Father loves us. This was something Paul understood when he said: 'My power is at its best in weakness' and 'It is when I am weak that I am strong' (2 Cor. 12:9 and 10). It is something described by George Herbert in his poem 'Love':

"Love bade me welcome: yet my soul drew back,
   Guiltie of dust and sinne.
But quick-ey'd Love, observing me grow slack

129

From my first entrance in,
Drew nearer to me, sweetly questioning,
If I lack'd any thing.

A guest, I answer'd, worthy to be here:
Love said, you shall be he.
I the unkinde, ungratefull? Ah my deare,
I cannot look on thee.
Love took my hand, and smiling did reply,
Who made the eyes but I?

Truth Lord, but I have marr'd them: let my shame
Go where it doth deserve.
And know you not, sayes Love, who bore the blame?
My deare, then I will serve.
You must sit down, sayes Love, and taste my meat:
So I did sit and eat."

Even when we have acknowledged our own sinfulness,
comprehend our need of forgiveness, and no longer
suffer from 'hardness of heart', however, we have not
yet explained how in Herbert's words Jesus 'bore the
blame', or how we are 'made perfect in weakness'. Since
the people of Israel on their annual Day of Atonement
recognized that, in addition to cleansing rituals, there
was need to despatch a scapegoat into the desert as a
symbolic sin-offering, it is even more imperative that as
Christians we discover how Jesus actually (as distinct
from symbolically) atoned for us.

Via Crucis
In response to a sceptic's questions, 'What was so special
about the death of Jesus on the cross?' and 'Haven't
countless other men and women throughout history

undergone even more agonizing deaths?', a priest once replied that, for a Christian, Jesus is not just anyone; he is the Son of God. The crucifixion of Jesus was not merely another instance in a catalogue of barbarous deaths down the centuries, nor simply an example of supreme altruism — though it was both. More importantly it was the pivotal point in what is known as salvation history. Naturally it was completely consonant with Jesus' whole outlook and behaviour; it was the climax of a life in which two themes predominated: that of total obedience to his Father's will, and that of utter self-giving. More significantly, however, the event on Calvary was the consummation of all that God had long prepared for in the way of restoring man to his favour. It was ratified by God when he raised Jesus from the dead.

For this reason alone, any type of Christianity which endeavours to play down the cross is necessarily truncated, shorn of its ultimate meaning, and bereft of its *raison d'être*. In the same way our worship and devotion, including our understanding of sin and efforts to obtain reconciliation, will be warped if we omit knowledge and experience of the cross. 'If anyone wants to be a follower of mine', said Jesus, 'let him renounce himself and take up his cross and follow me' (Mk 8:34).

The significant difference between Jesus' death and that of all other men was pointed out by Jesus himself when he spoke of giving his life as 'a ransom for many' (Mk 10:45); and at the Last Supper when he uttered the memorable words: 'This cup is the new covenant in my blood which will be poured out for you'.

It is this dimension to his death, known as the act of atonement (at-one-ment), which we need to grasp; without it we would still be a people without hope (1 Cor. 15:12-19); had it not occurred, man's alienation from

131

God and his thraldom to sin would remain. Of ourselves we could not achieve reconciliation and, out of love, 'It was God who reconciled us to himself through Christ' (2 Cor. 5:18). Such indeed was the magnitude of what happened that first Good Friday, that theologians down the ages have endeavoured to explain it. And the Church in its wisdom has never declared any one of their ideas to be the only official formulation of how Jesus did in fact redeem us.

The most important exposition of the doctrine of atonement is found in St Paul. Not only did Paul regard Jesus' death and resurrection as the means by which man is liberated and redeemed from the effects of sin, but he went on to preach that by baptism the Christian mystically shares in Jesus' death and victory over it. In other words, through baptism an individual acquires a new status of sonship of justification before God. The Easter events had an objectivity of their own, but at the same time and through faith they are able to bear fruit in the life of a believer. Both these aspects need to be borne in mind, even though the present intention is to explore more fully how 'through the blood of his cross' (Col. 1:20) Jesus made peace between God and man; that aspect of his death known in technical language as a propitiation and found also in the teaching of Peter: 'Remember, the ransom that was paid to free you from the useless way of life your ancestors handed down was not paid in anything corruptible, neither in silver nor gold, but in the precious blood of a lamb without spot or stain, namely Christ' (1 Pet. 1:18-19).

Precisely how Jesus ransomed us was a theme frequently debated by the early Fathers of the Church. Origen (c.185-c.254), for instance, considered Jesus' death to be a ransom paid to Satan who had obtained rights over man from the time of man's first disobedience. Later this view was taken up, adapted and taught by such men as Hilary of Poitiers, Augustine and Leo; all of them were careful, however, to point out that Satan in his turn was conquered by the power of the resurrection.

A modern version of this theory is to be found in what is sometimes only regarded as a book suitable for children: *The Lion, the Witch and the Wardrobe,* the first volume of the Narnia stories by C.S. Lewis. It is only with difficulty that any adult can restrain himself from sharing in the sorrow experienced by children when he reads of the lion Aslan going voluntarily and sadly to his torture and death at the hands of the witch, surrounded by her minions in the shape of ogres, wolves, bull-headed men and hosts of other evil creatures. When dawn broke the following morning, however, and the great Stone Table on which Aslan had met his death cracked in two, Aslan appeared before his friends in a glorious manner. The parallel with Jesus' death and resurrection becomes clear. Aslan then explained the meaning of all this to his astonished human friends: 'It means', said Aslan, 'that though the Witch knew the Deep Magic, there is a magic deeper still which she did not know. Her knowledge goes back only to the dawn of time. But if she could have looked a little further back, into the stillness and the darkness before Time dawned, she would have read there a different incantation. She would have known that when a willing victim who had committed no treachery was killed in a traitor's stead, the Table would crack and Death itself would start working backwards'.

In the language of the early Fathers, however, and with reference to what occurred on Calvary, Jesus is mankind's representative not substitute; and the effects of Jesus' work extend to the whole of humanity and beyond.

The appearance at the end of the eleventh century of St Anselm's study, *Cur Deus Homo,* besides being an immense contribution to the theology of the atonement, marked a change in emphasis and a shift away from ideas which had hitherto held the field. Anselm repudiated the rôle of Satan in regard to the cross. He substituted the idea of satisfaction, for, according to him, since sin was an infinite offence against God, it required a satisfaction equally infinite. For Anselm the death of Jesus was not a ransom paid to the devil but a debt paid to the Father. It was this theory of satisfaction which dominated western Christian thinking until the Reformation, having been accepted though modified by Aquinas to exclude any idea that the particular method by which we were redeemed, saved or reconciled was imperative. According to Aquinas, God could have redeemed us without exacting full satisfaction, though in the event the satisfaction proved superabundant.

The next major interpretation of what precisely took place on Calvary came from the Reformers. Whilst accepting much of what had become by the time of the Reformation the traditional view of atonement, Martin Luther for instance inserted the notion of voluntary substitution into his teaching on the subject, in place of the theory of satisfaction. In simple language, Luther taught that Jesus, by bearing the punishment due to man, was reckoned by God to be a sinner in his place. John Calvin conceived an even more radical version of atonement by maintaining that Jesus 'bore in his soul the tortures of a condemned and ruined man'.

Inevitably many considered such theories too 'penal' or found that they emphasized unduly the idea of punishment; for others they evoked too much the notion of an unjust God; and, in their reaction against them, such sects as the Socinians or Unitarians preferred to propagate the idea that Jesus died as he did only as an example to his followers.

In modern times, largely owing to the influence of the Scandinavian Gustav Aulén, the author of *Christus Victor,* there has been a return to the version of the atonement associated with the early Fathers, sometimes referred to as the 'classic' view. This has the advantage of being deeply rooted in the New Testament. There the cross is depicted as summing up the life and work of Jesus in all their totality, and as a victory over all the enticements that enslave man. This view has the additional advantage of conveying how the event on Calvary was objective, an event in its own right, something done on behalf of man, and at the same time subjective, an example of complete love for man to imitate.

In the words of Paul, 'God has delivered us from the kingdom of darkness and transferred us to the kingdom of his beloved Son' (Col. 1:13). He has broken the hold of the evil powers over us by 'nailing it to the cross' (Col. 2:14). And, 'He disarmed the principalities and powers and made a public example of them, triumphing over them in him' (Col. 2:15).

Whereas it is relatively easy to see the cross as an example of obedience and utter self-giving, and thereby as something for all Christians to follow, the reality of atonement goes deeper. In order to penetrate to an understanding of how Jesus triumphed and in what ways his victory continues, it is necessary to explore more deeply the nature of sacrifice and what the author of the Epistle to the Hebrews describes as the high-priestly rôle of Jesus.

From at least the time of Aaron, the people of Israel had always viewed the task of priests as acting for men in their relations with God and offering gifts and sacrifices for sin (Heb. 5:1). They differentiated clearly between priests and prophets. They recognized in this their need for something to be done *for* them, something which they were impotent of themselves to do. What was still needed however was what Jesus was: namely, 'the ideal high priest . . . holy, innocent and uncontaminated . . . one who would not need to offer sacrifices every day, as the other high priests do for their own sins and then for those of the people, because he has done this once and for all, by offering himself' (Heb. 7:26-27). And this Jesus did for man on the cross. On Calvary Jesus was both the new high priest and victim. This act of total self-giving in character with his whole life and work was so dynamic and divine that its effects could not be confined to one single Friday almost 2000 years ago.

Following Karl Barth in his campaign to place the cross rather than the manger of Bethlehem at the centre of our faith, perhaps the most succinct recent account of what occurred that first Easter has come from A.M. Hunter in his book *Jesus, Lord and Saviour*. As a worthy successor to the Protestant giants of the Reformation it is not surprising that Dr Hunter should have turned his mind to the punishment aspect of Jesus' passion'. '"Penal" Christ's sufferings were', says Hunter, 'but only in the sense that in his passion he had to endure on men's behalf the divine reaction against the sin of the human race to whom, as the Son of Man, he had betrothed himself, for better or worse . . . We may . . . perceive that, in so identifying himself with sinners, he was honouring the holiness of God who, just because of his love for them, cannot palter with sin but must deal with it decisively, if men are to be forgiven'.

Quoting another writer, Hunter adds that Christ as

our representative, offered on the cross a perfect confession of our sins, a confession which could be described
as 'a perfect Amen in humanity to the judgment of God
on the sin of man'.

Such is the wonderful mystery of the cross, however,
that it is likely to continue defying any attempt to
explain it to everyone's intellectual satisfaction. This
does not excuse us nevertheless from constantly medi-
tating upon it, or from seeking to experience its
continuing effects in our daily lives.

As the author of the Epistle to the Hebrews said, it
was 'once and for all'. In another sense it continues to
be re-presented every day — as for instance, most
supremely, in the eucharist. Moreover, whenever
Christians respond with faith to the sacrament and
accept it as God's method of reconciling man, then not
only do we know what Jesus did for us but we experience
how he works in us still. The cross is both past and
present. Herein lies one of the many paradoxes to be
discovered in God's dealings with man.

To modern man it may be that such beliefs and
practices are not merely perplexing but seem even outmoded. In a technological era such as our own, however,
the possibilities of enslavement to sin, or of becoming
obsessed with things and even ideas which estrange us
from God, our neighbour and our true selves, are
arguably even more numerous than ever before. This is
the modern temptation to worship idols. Whereas in the
Old Testament the Jews at times were castigated for
worshipping false gods ('They sacrificed to demons
which were no gods, to gods they had never known, to
new gods that had come in of late, whom your fathers
had never dreaded. You were unmindful of the Rock
that begot you, and you forgot the God who gave you

137

birth' [Deut. 32:17-18]), is modern man that much different? Our need of reconciliation at the hands of Christ may indeed be greater, so more than ever we need to penetrate and interiorize the work of Christ on behalf of man summed up by Paul's message to the Romans, the fruit of which is have glory as our destiny: 'If it is certain', wrote Paul, 'that through one man's fall so many died, it is even more certain that divine grace, coming through the one man, Jesus Christ, came to so many as an abundant free gift. The results of the gift also outweigh the results of one man's sin: for after one single fall came judgment with a verdict of condemnation, now after many falls comes grace with its verdict of acquittal. If it is certain that death, reigned over everyone as the consequence of one man's fall, it is even more certain that one man, Jesus Christ, will cause everyone to reign in life who receives the free gift that he does not deserve, of being made righteous. Again, as one man's fall brought condemnation on everyone, so the good act of one man brings everyone life and makes them justified. As by one man's disobedience many were made sinners, so by one man's obedience many will be made righteous' (Rom. 5:15-20).

Further reading (Part II)

Charles Curran, *A New Look at Christian Morality* (London, 1976)

Charles Curran, *Contemporary Problems in Moral Theology* (Indiana, 1970)

A.M. Hunter, *The Parables, Then and Now* (London, 1971)

A.M. Hunter, *Jesus, Lord and Saviour* (London, 1976)

C.S. Lewis, *Voyage to Venus* (London, 1968)

C.S. Lewis, *The Lion, the Witch and the Wardrobe* (London, 1974)

John Macquarrie, *Principles of Christian Theology* (London, 1970)

Edward Matthews, *The Forgiveness of Sins* (London, 1978)

Thomas Merton, *Elected Silence* (London, 1948)

Thomas Merton, *Seeds of Contemplation* (London, 1972)

Thomas Merton, *No Man is an Island* (London, 1974)

Louis Monden, *Sin, Liberty and Law* (London, 1969)

Sister Lawrence Murray, *Confession: Outmoded Sacrament?* (London, 1972)

J.H. Newman, *Certain Difficulties Felt by Anglicans in Catholic Teaching* (London, 1876)

Rudolf Schnackenburg, *The Moral Teaching of the New Testament* (London, 1975)

KARL RAHNER

CHRISTIAN AT THE CROSSROADS

In this important new book for Christians in an age of un-
certainty, Karl Rahner speaks from profound knowledge of
the faith and with rare sensitivity to the mood of the times.
We are at the cross-roads. We have to ask the really important
questions with unusual care and responsibility: What is man?
What is truth? What does being a Christian mean? What are
prayer and penance? What is the right attitude to the enigma
of death? We have to inquire into the age-old problems with
a new urgency. Yet this is an urgency not of desperation but
of unfailing hope that we will come through despite everything.
Here one of the great theologians of the century reaches the
heart of the average Christian, yet with an assurance of style
and thought that never shirks the hard questions of the
theologian. These are words of the spirit intended to point out
not just one way ahead, but the right frame of mind and the
right things to ask when choosing that way.

ENCOUNTERS WITH SILENCE

This is one of Karl Rahner's most direct and powerful books.
It is also one of the most loving and lucid of his works. It is a
book of meditations about man's relationship with God. It is
not a work of dry theology, but a book of prayerful reflections
on love, knowledge and faith, obedience, everyday routine,
life with our friends and neighbours, our work and vocation,
and human goodness. The immense success of this moving
work is a tribute to its practicality and the ability of the great
theologian to speak simply and yet profoundly to the ordinary
man or woman seeking an inspiring guide for the inner life
that never forsakes the world of reality. The book is cast in
the form of a dialogue with God that moves from humble but
concerned inquiry to joyful contemplation. It fully deserves
its reputation as one of the classics of modern spirituality.

THE NEW MAN

Thomas Merton

Thomas Merton is one of very few writers on the spiritual life who can speak to men in the present age in a language they can understand. *The New Man* is probably the most important work of the mature Merton. It is about living the full life of a Christian in a world that is increasingly out of touch with real humanity as it is out of touch with God. Merton is concerned with our knowing who we really are and what we must do if we want to find our true selves again. 'It is a spiritual disaster', he says, 'for a man to rest content with his exterior identity, with his passport picture of himself . . . . Since we are made in the image and likeness of God, there is no other way to find out who we are than by finding, in ourselves, the divine image'. To this theme of the true nature of man Merton joins an exploration of the attitude contrary to the Christian and summarizes it by applying the Prometheus myth to the present age: 'Prometheus is the mystic without faith, who believes neither in himself nor in God. . . . the man who needs fire from outside himself is in a certain sense condemned to live out his life in the hope of some impossible ecstasy'. *The New Man* is a powerful and moving meditation on Christian renewal and a profound analysis of the loneliness and despair that lie within so many of the alternatives to God pursued by men today: 'The brightness of the eternal light is so great that we cannot see it, and all other lights become darkness by comparison with it. Yet to the spiritual man, all other lights contain the infinite light. He passes through them to reach it . . . instructed by the Spirit who alone can tell us the secret of our individual destiny, man begins to know God as he knows himself'.

LETTERS FROM THE DESERT

Charles de Foucauld

During the seven unforgettable years spent at Our Lady of the Snows the great spiritual thinker and writer carried on a profound and fascinating correspondence with his superiors and brothers in Christ. This selection of the most important letters of that period of trial, discovery, spiritual ardour and inspiring example has only recently been made available in the original French and now appears in English for the first time. This is a publishing event for all those who follow the desert way. Here is the very heart of de Foucauld's spirituality: springs of refreshment in the desert, a simple yet ardent spirit wrestling with problems, questing and receiving comfort at decisive moments in a destiny of loving unity with Jesus.

HEY YOU!

Michael Hollings

This is probably Michael Hollings's most valuable book to date. It is a simple straightforward appeal to the very ordinary lay man and woman really to do something about prayer — both private and public. The author, who was a Guards officer before becoming a priest, writes in a virile modern idiom to the modern world about age-old truths. He is fully aware of the difficulties both of starting and persevering with prayer but he deals with the matter bluntly yet encouragingly. The first section of the book is concerned with the why and wherefore of prayer; the second with the example of prayer in the liturgy and the Mass — an account which is often enlivened with the author's personal knowledge of the Holy Places, or his experience of the stigmatic Padre Pio. The simplicity and sincerity which mark the author's approach and style cannot fail to win a response in the hearts of his readers — even those who would normally fight shy of a book dealing with prayer and the spiritual life. It will be a challenge to the indifferent and a stimulus to those who are finding the going hard.

THE LIVING BREAD

Thomas Merton

This book is a series of moving and resonant meditations on Christianity as Christ himself living in unity with men of good will. *The Living Bread* is a lasting exposition of the central truth of the Eucharist as the sacrament of love. This is no dull doctrinal compendium but a powerful document of the spirit asserting the unmistakable relevance of eternal truth to the present moment: 'The whole problem of our time is the problem of love. How are we going to recover the ability to love ourselves and to love one another? . . . We cannot be at peace with others because we are not at peace with ourselves, and we cannot be at peace with ourselves because we are not at peace with God . . . . Modern dictatorships display everywhere a deliberate and calculated hatred for human nature as such. The techniques of degradation used in concentration camps and in staged trials are too familiar in our time. They have one purpose: to defile the human person . . . . Passive and despairing, we allow ourselves to sink back into the inert mass of human objects that only exist to be manipulated by dictators, or by the great anonymous powers that rule the world of business . . . . To find God one must first be free . . . . To conquer the forces of death and despair, we must unite ourselves mystically to Christ who has overcome death and who brings us life and hope . . . . This book is not a defence of a doctrine, but a meditation on a sacred mystery'.